FEELING

The Educators' Guide for Eating Better, Exercising Smarter, and Feeling Your Best

Todd Whitaker

Jason Winkle

EYE ON EDUCATION
6 DEPOT WAY WEST, SUITE 106
LARCHMONT, NY 10538
(914) 833–0551
(914) 833–0761 fax
www.eyeoneducation.com

Library of Congress Cataloging-in-Publication Data

Whitaker, Todd, 1959–
    Feeling great! : the educator's guide for eating better, exercising smarter, and feeling your best / Todd Whitaker, Jason Winkle.
        p.   cm.
    Includes bibliographical references.
    ISBN 1-930556-38-1
    1. Teachers—Health and hygiene. 2. Teachers—Nutrition. 3. Physical fitness. I. Winkle, Jason M., 1969– . II. Title.
    LB3415.W45 2002
    613.7'024'372—dc21
                                                                            2002019511

10 9 8 7 6

Editorial and production services provided by
Richard H. Adin Freelance Editorial Services
52 Oakwood Blvd., Poughkeepsie, NY 12603-4112
(845-471-3566)

ABOUT THE AUTHORS

Dr. Todd Whitaker is a professor of educational leadership at Indiana State University in Terre Haute, Indiana. Prior to coming to Indiana, he was a middle- and high-school principal for eight years in Missouri. In addition, Dr. Whitaker served as middle-school coordinator in Jefferson City, Missouri, where he supervised all aspects of building, staffing, curriculum, programs, and technology of two new middle schools.

Dr. Whitaker has published in the areas of principal effectiveness, teacher leadership, change, staff motivation, instructional improvement, and middle-level practices. His previous books include *Dealing with Difficult Teachers, Motivating & Inspiring Teachers,* and *Dealing with Difficult Parents (And with Parents in Difficult Situations).* His other current book is *Teaching Matters: Motivating and Inspiring Yourself.* He is a highly sought speaker for teachers and principals. He has made hundreds of state, national, and international presentations.

Jason Winkle is a faculty member in the department of physical education at the United States Military Academy in West Point, New York. Prior to teaching at West Point, he was a faculty member at Indiana State University where he taught classes in fitness, organization and administration, and the martial arts. As a manager of Indiana State University's health clubs, Mr. Winkle supervised the daily operations of three facilities, and coordinated the aerobic and martial arts programs.

Mr. Winkle's previous books include *Kali: Weapon and Weaponless Self-Defense, Jeet Kune Do Concepts,* and *Teaching Martial Arts for Fun and Fitness: A Non-Contact Approach for Young People.* He travels the country speaking on fitness, leadership, and the martial arts to schools, businesses, and military and law enforcement agencies.

TABLE OF CONTENTS

THE WAY
WE SEE IT

The importance of educators can never be overstated. Without teachers, there would be no other professions. The willingness of people in this most caring profession to give of themselves is without equal. However, this book is not about giving even more of yourself. There are myriad resources encouraging you to do that. This book is about giving more *to* yourself. As teachers, professors, principals, and other professional educators, you spend so much time and energy being concerned about everyone else, that sometimes you may forget to turn that attention internally, to yourself. We know you work very hard making others feel great; we want to make sure that you have the privilege of knowing how it feels for *you* to feel great!

We know that there are literally hundreds of books, magazine articles, and quick-fix remedies that all purport to make you healthy. We know that the resources to exercise your way to a perfect body are available in seemingly unlimited quantities. However, one thing we often ask ourselves is, "Why don't they ever have pictures of anybody normal in those journals?"

Our goal is not to focus on you being the perfect physical specimen. Though, to paraphrase Jerry Seinfeld, there is nothing wrong with that. Instead, the goal of this book is similar to the goal of education. That is, we are hoping to help everyone be a little bit better than they were when they started. In writing this book, just as in teaching, we are in the improvement business, not the perfection business.

This book was written with every educator in mind. We are not attempting to help people become professional models or qualify for the Olympic marathon. Instead, what we are hoping to accomplish is provide the encouragement and the direction for everyone to do something that will improve their fitness. We are strong believers that the biggest gain isn't in increasing the amount of miles you jog. It isn't in changing your diet so that you lower your body fat from 8.6 to 8.3 percent. Though these may be positive goals and achievements for someone, somewhere, the real benefit is in moving from nothing to something. If *everyone* sets aside a small piece of their most precious of commodities, time, to focus on their physical selves, we will have accomplished our goals.

In this book, we encourage all educators to put themselves first—maybe for the first time in a long time. If you are a teacher, we want you! Your current age, weight, condition, and stamina make no difference. No matter where you are, we want to work together to make you an even better person. The body, mind, and spirit gain so much collectively when we take care of each of the parts. We can all remember when we felt and looked our best. Those were times when we had even more energy to give to others.

Is it even possible, given the many demands each of us face personally and professionally, to find the time to exercise regularly? How can I possibly have a healthy diet? Not only do I eat school lunches, I eat them in two minutes while I am standing up! We are well aware how valuable time is for every teacher and how many directions we are all pulled. The frenetic pace is something that all educators face. One of the biggest differences between education and other professions is the intensity in our jobs. Not only do we have nightly papers to grade and activities to supervise, we can't even get a 20 minute uninterrupted time at any point during the day. All of us have struggled to even work in a time to visit the bathroom! In order to meet these daily challenges, we must all discover ways to overcome our biggest obstacle—ourselves!

Understanding the importance of finding some time to take care of yourself and maybe even more critical is finding the will to make yourself do it is an essential part of being a well rounded person. The efforts to combine the essential role and demands placed on educators with the knowledge of how to work "smarter, not harder" is at the core of this book. We are confident that we can give you that one extra incentive, idea, or resource that will encourage you to help refocus on yourself.

Of course your students deserve the best you. And, maybe even more essentially, your family deserves the best you. However, regardless of your professional obligations and exclusive of your family make up, we know that YOU deserves the best you. This book will help you get on that wonderful road toward Feeling Great!

We are well aware of the tremendous demands facing everyone reading this book. To write a book that addresses your needs and interests, we are combining the resources of a former teacher and principal with those of a person who has devoted his life to fitness.

Jason Winkle is recognized as one of the leading martial arts experts in the world. He has helped train members of military Special Forces units, the U.S. Army, numerous law enforcement agencies, and hundreds of individuals. However, his work with "regular" people who are not in jobs that are so physically reliant may be some of his best work. Being able to determine things that everyone can, and even more importantly, *will* do may be his greatest challenge and most satisfying accomplishment. Working with many people whose livelihood and possibly their lives are reliant on their top physical condition is a very satisfying role; but being able to meet the needs of each individual he works with is equally rewarding.

Todd Whitaker is an average athlete who is pretty much self-taught just through stubbornness and a desire to lose weight. However, as a teacher and principal he was able to see the tremendous demands that are placed on educators every day. From his own experience, he was able to see the benefits for everyone in education of being able to exercise regularly and feeling good about themselves.

PART I

WHY SHOULD I BOTHER?

1

WHY FITNESS FOR EDUCATORS? WHAT'S SO SPECIAL ABOUT US?

Teachers, professors, principals, counselors, and everyone else associated with education thinks of themselves as in a giving profession. And, there is no question, we are correct in thinking that way. However, one of the challenges we face when we continually think about helping others is that we often forget to take care of ourselves. And, as educators, if we do not take care of ourselves, then we have much less ability to take care of those around us. There are many different ways to take care of ourselves. These include reading something uplifting or even watching a movie that cheers us up. Anything that helps your personal morale is valuable. The book *Teaching Matters: Motivating and Inspiring Yourself* is very insightful in supporting your emotional side. Yet, possibly the area we most ignore, is our physical self.

If we feel good about ourselves physically, it is amazing how much of a boost this gives us emotionally. And, by the same token, when we don't feel good about ourselves physically, it seems as if our whole world is less fun. The focus of this book is to help people in the most challenging, demanding, and stressful profession find the time in their busy lives to increase their energy, enthusiasm, and love for life. This book will help you look and feel your best so that you can always be your best for your students, your family, and most importantly, for yourself.

GETTING STARTED

On July 4th, 1981, I was at my girlfriend's family reunion picnic. Her family was very athletic, and so the entire day was centered about sports and competition. We had volleyball matches, softball games, and horseshoe challenges throughout the day. And, like all such summer gatherings, there was plenty of food and drink. Every time we had a chance, I grabbed another hotdog and a soda from the cooler. Just about every time we changed sides in volleyball or each time we came in to bat from the softball field, I would grab another handful of chips and make sure I washed it down with a cola. It was about 95 degrees out and it was typical Missouri humidity. Though I was having a great time, by the end of the day I was miserable. It wasn't the heat. It was from being exhausted from the games and it was mostly from feeling terrible about how much I had stuffed myself all day.

I remember feeling down about myself; and that evening, I was even feeling down about feeling down about myself! Then I took a look in the mirror that night and I decided I just had to do something about my appearance. This wasn't the first time I felt that way. I had jogged for two or three days in a row a couple of times over the last five years. Once in a while I even watched what I ate for two consecutive meals. And, for several years, I had been concerned because my dad had a heart attack five years before that, when I was in high school, and I did not want that to happen to me. So, I finally decided to do something about it. And I decided that July 5th would be the day.

There was no *Rocky* soundtrack in the background and it was another scorcher outside, but when I got on the scale at a robust 215 that morning I decided that I had had enough. And I realized that the biggest thing holding me back was my own ego. It sounds funny, but because I did not like the way I looked at that time in street clothes, I realized that I was even more self-conscious of my appearance when exercising. This always provided me another disincentive or excuse not to work on improving my physical fitness. Thus, for years, I only would do things when no one could see me. I did not want to be out jogging and hear someone yell, "It's about time!" But, finally, I decided that regardless of what anyone was going to say to me or about me, I was going to do it for me.

So that afternoon I laced up my only pair of sneakers— some worn out basketball shoes I had—and I decided that I was going to run this little course near my house. I decided that I was not going to care what I looked like, I was going to do it for me. And, I made a commitment for myself that I did not care how fast I went—or how *slow* I went!—but I was not going to stop until I was back home. And, miracle upon miracle, I did it. I was sore, I was exhausted, but I did it. I was proud, but very stiff. But I made a commitment to myself that I was going to do the same thing, no matter what, the next day.

On July 6th, I did not want to get out of bed, much less go jogging. However, I had made a promise to myself that I would do it. And that day I realized one of the biggest keys for me to exercise. I have to remember what I feel like when I am done before I ever start. As we discuss in Chapter 3, the first step is almost always the hardest. If we can trick ourselves into starting, it is much easier to do the rest. So, I forced myself to recall how good it felt when I was done yesterday so that I could start again today.

I trudged around my little 2.3-mile circle that afternoon and was even slower than I was the day before. I am sure that if anyone, young or old, had been out walking at the same time, they would have readily passed me. However, I kept my promise and did not stop.

I think because my normally dormant body was rebelling against the exercise, I even didn't really feel like eating much. Probably a combination of the jogging and the heat, I thought. It was funny, but I felt kind of proud after only two days. The next day I laced up the old shoes and did it again.

After a few days, *I realized how much it was all up to me.* And, how much it had *always* been up to me to take care of myself. I reflected back and it dawned on me how much my physical self really was a choice. I had just been choosing to not take care of myself. It truly was up to me to decide each day what I wanted that day to be like.

I began to eat better and continued to go out and jog my little path no matter what the weather. I did not allow myself to have any excuses. Eventually my pants felt more comfortable and before too long they were even loose! Clothes that I had not been able to wear in years now were sliding off me.

I continued to jog—some days I would even do my little circle twice in a day—and most of the time I watched what I ate. When graduate school started again that fall, people who had not seen me since the spring could not believe it! By October I had lost 49 pounds and never felt better! This is where my interest in taking care of myself physically came from. I had mindlessly made myself do something, *anything*, positive for myself. It became a habit and when we make positive changes in our appearance, it becomes reinforcing in and of itself.

However, I still did not know what I was doing, and the diet I was on was probably not the best. Then someone lent me a copy of Jim Fixx's classic, *The Complete Book of Running* (New York: Random House, 1977). It inspired me, true, but more importantly, it gave me some direction. I realized that I needed better shoes (those old hightops were worn to a frazzle by now) and how essential it is to warm up and stretch. The book also helped me understand how to build jogging into my schedule and make it work for me.

IT HAS TO WORK FOR YOU

I was not a particularly good athlete in school. Although I played some sports, my conditioning was always limited to whatever we had to do at the start of the season. Once I got into college, I quickly succumbed to the "freshman 15" and gained my 15 pounds by the end of my first semester. Gradually, I became less and less active and less and less happy with the way I looked.

However, I realized that when I started to exercise that not only did I lose weight, I also felt much better about myself. My energy level was higher and I had a much more positive frame of mind. I could sleep more soundly, and maybe more importantly, the worries of the world became much less imposing.

For years thereafter as a teacher and a principal, I would try to always exercise in the morning. It is amazing what that did for me. It allowed me to regularly be excited to go to school. I was wide awake and ready for the challenges that we all face. I can remember wondering why everyone else wasn't in a good mood. I really could tell if I ever missed a day of exercise. I was less patient, much more tired, and looked at the world in a glass-half-empty frame of mind when I had not exercised in the morning.

I remember when I became a middle-school principal. If I exercised, even just a little, before I came to work, the potential of facing a disgruntled parent didn't seem nearly as demanding. Exercise and taking care of myself truly changed my life.

LEARNING HOW, LEARNING BETTER

I am reminded of a track coach that was at a middle school where I was principal. I remember in particular how this coach used to address athletes at track practice and at the meets. No matter who was running, this coach always used to yell, "Run faster!"

Now, I am not a track expert, but I have great confidence that these middle-school students were running as fast as they knew how. Yelling "run faster" probably was not going to accomplish anything. Instead, what they needed was to learn *how* to run faster.

This book will assist you in doing all of the things you already know that you should be doing. The goal is to help you do them better and hopefully to inspire you to do them more regularly.

We all know we should watch what we eat. Everyone is aware that exercising regularly is important. And, everyone wants to look and feel their best. We are not going to remind you that these things are important. Instead, we will work to help all educators to do these things even better. And, we will assist you in being able to fit them into the complex schedule and demanding occupation that you have.

You are in a giving profession and spend your life being selfless and giving to others. This is very commendable and something to be tremendously proud of. You have chosen to devote your professional life to helping others. There is nothing more important you can do as a career.

However, we do have one favor to ask you. While you read this book, we would like you to not do what is in it for your students, for your supervisor, or even for your family. We would like for you to do it for the most important person in your life—you. You are worth it.

2

WHAT, ME A MODEL?
NO, A ROLE MODEL!

One of our core beliefs as educators is that every day students watch all of our actions. Whether our actions are kind or intolerant, positive or sarcastic, with every thing we do, students observe and learn from us. Sometimes they learn good things that we would like them to emulate, and other times we would rather they practice the old adage, "Do what I say, not what I do." Though that is an easy saying to recite, if there is a conflict between our actions and our dialogue, it is much more likely that students will do as we do rather than as we say. Hopefully though, these two things are usually consistent. When this occurs, the chances of students seeing us, hearing us, and duplicating us are much greater. Being aware of the importance of our actions, maybe more so than our words, may help us in our efforts to care for ourselves.

A second core focus of this book is that there is no one best way to diet or exercise. If there were, everyone would be doing it. You may need to write down and keep track of specific goals. You may need to continually set short-term goals so that you can maintain needed incentives. Whatever you find that works for you is great. We need to celebrate any reasons that encourage us to begin and continue our self-help programs. This is especially true for the many selfless people who have chosen to devote their lives to others as educators. Because we are so often centered on the needs of others, it is easy to minimize our own personal needs. But even if your focus is primarily on others, you can turn that outward focus into motivation to work on yourself. Here are a couple of reasons that thinking about the needs of your students may allow you to, at the same time, meet the needs of yourself.

EVEN IF YOU DON'T WANT
TO DO IT FOR YOURSELF

A major theme of this book is that we need to take care of ourselves so that we have more ability to take care of others. In a giving profession, perhaps the *most* giving profession, educators consistently put the needs of others ahead of their own. This is okay and even admirable, up to a point. However, as we mentioned in Chapter 1, if we don't take care of ourselves, we will not be there to take care of anyone else either. This is a mantra that will be repeated throughout this book. However, let's take just a minute and think of others again.

If you are among the thousands of selfless educators, congratulations. The students you meet are much better off in knowing and working with you. Because of this, it may be harder for you than it is for others to set aside time and opportunities to focus on yourself. Maybe your feeling of guilt that there is always more you can be doing for your students, your school, or your family tend to dominate even the rare chances you have for self-improvement. Well, if this describes you, then we encourage you to use your concern for others as a motivation to be more selfish. It may sound contradictory, but let's think of it this way....

One of the most important gifts we could ask for our students and our own children is for them to have good physical health. Though we know genetics and other factors come into play, there is still much that everyone can do to take control of their own bodies. We can educate our students about nutrition. We can assign materials in our classes regarding the values and benefits of regular exercise. If we teach physical education, we might even be able to require students to do things that can improve their fitness level for the near term. However, if our goal is to develop positive lifelong health, then the best way to get that integrated into their personal habits and belief systems is to practice it ourselves. This will help align our actions with our words and be much more likely to carry over into the lives of the young people we live and work with. Like the saying goes, "If we don't model what we teach, then we are teaching something else."

If continuing to focus on your core need and belief in helping others actually frees up your conscious enough to allow you to find the time to exercise more regularly, then by all means tap into your guilt pool so that you can do what is right. No matter who you are exercising and dieting for, your heart probably doesn't know the difference. If you would like your children to grow up with healthy parents, then this may allow you to rationalize setting aside time each week to exercise. If you would like your children to lead healthy lifestyles themselves, then one of the best things you could do is live your own life in a positive manner. Knowing that if you lead a healthy lifestyle, they are more likely to also, may help give you the incentive needed to do what is best for you. Not only is this a valuable gift you can give others, it may be the most valuable gift you can give yourself. And, in the long run, it is what is best for your children and the students you work with.

BUT I AM NO ATHLETE

Often we may think of dieting as something for skinny people and exercise for something that natural athletes do. As we know, adults vary greatly when it comes to coordination and body shape. And, maybe even more so, so do the students we work with. And, the authors believe that the less of a natural athlete we are, the more valuable we may be as a role model when we exercise. And, by the same token, the more we may struggle with our own weight, when we reflect a personal belief about eating in a healthy manner, we may even more positively influence our students.

Many times, students who are athletic come from families who are more gifted physically. And, the opposite is also true. If we think about our least physically fit and most inactive students, they need positive role models more than any others. If they see adults who may have similar natural make ups exercising and making conscious positive decisions about why they choose to do it, it may allow them to feel more comfortable in taking care of themselves. Students are more likely to be drawn to and emulate teachers that they can relate to. Sometimes it is because they share common interests. Often it is because those teachers give them a valuable gift—attention. And maybe it is because they see a little of themselves in their teachers. If all of us, regardless of shape, size, and natural fitness level can work on improving ourselves, then we can impact the wide variety of students that we work with.

If only the two or three most fit adults in a school exercise and watch what they eat, then many students who do not share the same body shape may not be able to draw on them for inspiration. Instead, if an entire faculty and staff, or even a large portion of them, at a school can each find some things that they are going to do to take care of themselves, then every student in the school can have someone that they might be likely to follow.

So, as contradictory as it might seem, possibly the most unfit teachers and staff members in a school can have the biggest impact on the students. Not only will these people potentially benefit more than any other adults in the schools as they improve their own health, it may cause the students most at risk for future health problems to also have the greatest benefit.

MAKE YOUR STUDENTS
AWARE OF WHAT YOU DO

I am reminded of a story that happened in a kindergarten class. It was a rainy day and at the start of class, the kindergarten teacher said, "Boys and girls, it was raining this morning when I was driving to work. Because of this, we probably will stay inside for recess."

A young boy in the back of the class, with a puzzled look on his face, raised his hand and asked the teacher, "Where do you work?"

Though this story may be a tribute to the teacher and how they never made teaching seem like work to their students, it probably also reflects how much students may not see us as real people. A friend of mine who was a teacher stopped off at the grocery store one day on her way home from school. When she was walking down the produce aisle, she ran into one of her middle-school students with his mom. The teacher said,

"Hello, Chris." And the stunned student looked up and replied, "What are *you* doing here?"

It is funny how the students often assume that we live at the school because we are there when they leave and there when they arrive the next morning. And, I am sure for all of us, at times we feel like we do!

Thus it is essential that not only do we choose to live a healthy lifestyle, but also that we make sure the students are aware that we do. When we make sure that all of the young people that we come in contact with understand how important we feel taking care of ourselves is, they can build these same beliefs about themselves.

Sharing things like, "When I was out walking this morning I thought to myself, 'what activities should we do in science class this week?'" or "Last night when I was debating whether or not to get dessert, I remembered what we had talked about in health class so I chose the sherbet rather than the sundae." Though these may seem like simple things, making sure that our students are aware of the choices we make and what we regularly do in the way of exercise can help them realize that is it an essential part of your life. This will assist in our efforts in making it a natural part of their lives as young people and maybe even more importantly, as they move into adulthood.

Whether we teach preschool or college, making sure that students are aware of the positive things we do in our personal lives for ourselves can be critical building blocks as they make their own choices. Also, by sharing ways that we motivate ourselves when we least feel like it, or showing them that we don't let one bad day cause us to throw in the towel on a healthy lifestyle, we can help our students build these same skills in themselves.

THE MOST IMPORTANT PERSON IN YOUR LIFE—YOU

Possibly the most important reason that we take care of ourselves is because we are worth it. Making sure that our students understand their own self-value is a critical skill to model and teach. We know that student self-esteem is highly correlated with teachers self-esteem (Lumpa, D. K. *Correlates with teacher and student satisfaction in elementary and middle schools*. Unpublished doctoral dissertation, University of Missouri, Columbia, MO, 1997). Helping the young people we come in contact with understand the things that we do to take care of themselves may allow them to be more aware of the importance of them taking care of themselves. And, when we feel better about ourselves, we treat those around us better. Having our students feel better about themselves and thus treat their peers and even their teachers with more kindness can in turn give us a selfish benefit.

Having happy, healthy, and productive students makes all of us feel more valuable as teachers. If assisting them to be healthier allows them to come to class in a more positive frame of mind, then this is just another reason why it is to our benefit. It is amazing what a positive circle we can establish by taking care of ourselves and assisting those around us to do the same.

So, if we really care for our students, and we have great faith that everyone reading this book does, then one more thing we can do for them is to show them the power of caring for ourselves. There may not be a greater treasure we can bestow those around us than this.

PART II

GETTING STARTED

3

THAT COOL-OF-THE-EVENING FEELING— REMEMBERING HOW YOU'LL FEEL WHEN YOU ARE DONE, BEFORE YOU EVEN START

One of our biggest challenges as we embark on a new exercise program is getting started. Perhaps an even bigger obstacle is continuing on the trek once we actually do get started. Finding a way that personally allows you to initiate an exercise program and then to sustain it is a challenge we all face. Though successful people have found things that work for them, your quest is to find a way that will assist *you* in being successful in meeting this goal.

THAT COOL-OF-THE-EVENING FEELING

I am not a big fan of mowing my lawn. I am not a big outdoors person, and if I really get down to it, I don't really like to sweat. Getting myself motivated to start up the lawn mower is always difficult for me. By the same token, I love having the yard freshly hewn. There is nothing better than the satisfaction and pride in having my lawn looking good—and knowing that I did not have to mess with it again. At least for a few days. There is nothing better than the feeling of accomplishment. When it comes to having the lawn mowed, I call it, "That cool-of-the-evening feeling."

When you feel satisfied with yourself, there is no better feeling. The sky looks bluer, the birds sound prettier, and even the lemonade tastes better. Well, that same feeling can and will be yours when you exercise. For me it is like getting motivated to mow the lawn. I just have to remember how I will feel when I am done, before I even start. If I fail to do so, I may never start and thus never get that great feeling of being done!

It is amazing, but no matter how tired I am, when I go and exercise, once I am done, my energy level is at a peak. The music is better, the sitcom is funnier, and that sport drink tastes even more satisfying. And, on some days, I just have to re-member how I will feel when I am done before I start. If I don't, then I find that often I never do begin.

Imagine how good it would feel to have that tense feeling in your shoulders just melt away. Wouldn't it be great to have a way to forget about your most challenging student, even if just for a while? How can I shift from my "work mode" to my "home mode"? The answer to each of these riddles is exercise. You know that once you get done working out, even if it is just for a few minutes, you will look at the world in a more positive light. If you can just remember that before you start, you are much more likely to get in the habit of making exercise a regu-lar part of your life.

THE FIRST STEP IS THE HARDEST

Educators are generally highly motivated. One of the traits of many teachers is that of being a high achiever. Often, how-ever, it seems that our lives are driven by guilt. Though this trait may help us be better professionally, it may also prevent us from devoting as much time and energy as we need in or-der to exercise regularly. Our level of guilt may make us feel that everything is up to us. If we do not do it, then it will not ever get done. Well, let us use this professional trait to assist us in our personal life.

I have great faith that everyone reading this book can walk one block, swim one lap, bike one block, or jog several feet. You might be thinking, "Sure, but what good will that do me?" Let's look at how that first step can lead us to a truly valuable and invigorating life change.

If you can make yourself start exercising, and by that I mean just taking the first few steps or pedaling a few feet, then often your guilt will kick in and you will not let yourself quit until you have had a more complete workout. But one thing is certain: there is no chance you will jog two miles until you take the first two steps. Make a promise to yourself that at the least you will exercise for five minutes on four days a week. If you take these very first steps and keep your promise to start, I have great faith that the same drive that makes you successful at work will many times take over and keep you moving for a positive workout. Whatever it is that works for you, is what you need to do.

One question that we also often ask ourselves is whether we should find an exercise partner or if it is best that we do an exercise program alone. The answer is very definitive. Whatever works best for you is what you should do. Let's look at some of the pros and the cons.

IS "ONE" THE LONELIEST NUMBER?

Through high school and college, whenever I would get discouraged enough about my weight or appearance to actually do something about it, I would scout around and try to find someone else who also felt sorry for themselves. Then, I would try to talk them into doing some type of a workout with me. I thought if I had a partner, it would keep me going on the days that I did not want to exercise. What I found was that the opposite was true for me.

Many people who exercise fairly regularly still come up with excuses now and then to skip a workout. If this does not become too much of a habit, there is nothing at all wrong with this. If letting yourself "off the hook" a couple of times a month keeps you going, then that is great. However, what I found with a partner is that now there were two of us to make excuses.

If every time I didn't want to work out I wouldn't, that is one thing. However, for me, I also discovered that in addition to my personally caused missteps, every time my partner wanted to skip, I also took the day off. Thus, two or three days a month quickly becomes four or six days a month. Eventually, it became 28 to 31 days a month! This is especially true if you find someone who is less committed and motivated then you are. But the opposite effect can also occur.

If you link up with a partner who is more motivated than you are, it may help sustain or possibly even increase your efforts. If being around someone more dedicated causes you to dip into your "guilt bucket" and make you more likely to exercise, then by all means, go for it. Tapping into someone else's commitment and drive can help expand your own capabilities. Then, if you keep focusing on how you will feel when you are done, and if you keep taking that first step, eventually you will be able to internalize the type of drive that your partner has in yourself.

And, if you are in a regular pattern and someone wants to tap into your energy, just make sure that they accommodate you rather than vice versa. If you have something that allows you to stay focused, then make sure you do not lose that energy by getting too far away from what works for you in order to assist someone else. That doesn't mean that those efforts are not gracious, but if you lose your own habits, then you no longer have the ability to aid your potential partners.

IT REALLY DOES GET EASIER

It may be hard to believe, but once you begin to get in shape it becomes easier and easier to exercise. As you lose weight, your body has less bulk to carry. If you would like to be reassured about this before you start, try this. If you want to know how much easier jogging will be after you lose 10 pounds, try jogging while carrying a 10-pound weight! Then, put it down and continue your trek. Quickly you will see that once you drop a little weight, jogging will get easier and easier. Just this simple truth may be enough to get you started.

The first four days are always the most challenging. After that, you begin to see the results and much of the original soreness evaporates. It also gets easier to focus on how you will feel once you are done simply because you have more positive feelings to tap into. It is hard to know how good it feels once you have completed mowing your yard if you have never mowed the yard. The more of these experiences you can develop, the more you have positive thoughts to fall back on in order to help you sustain your efforts.

THE EXERCISE TRADE-OFF

Another way to help sustain your exercise routine is to tell yourself that you can enjoy that dessert when you go out to eat tonight if you bike an extra mile or swim two more laps. Not only will this give your program a boost, it will actually make that piece of peanut butter pie taste that much better—if for no other reason, then perhaps because it won't be tainted with guilt!

Any or all of the ideas may work for you. The key is finding out what is the best fit. If linking up with someone else is helpful, that is great. Maybe mixing in combination and solo workouts with some partner pairing is best for you. Tricking yourself by agreeing to jog one block may seem like a silly way to start, but if that aids in your efforts to jog a mile, then by all means do it.

Your personal health and well-being are so essential that any approach you take is what you need to do. My personal favorite was to always exercise first thing in the morning. Not only was it wonderful to have it done for the day, but I could also have jogged the first two miles before I even realized what I was doing. This may not exactly be true, but until I figured out a personal fit, I was never going to become more personally fit. Good luck figuring our what works best for you.

SET A TIME LIMIT

One idea that can be successful in developing exercise into a routine is to exercise by time. What this means is to set a certain time limit for exercising that can serve as a minimum, maximum, or both.

Setting a minimum of say, 30 minutes, can actually give us more freedom when we exercise and can prevent monotony. A personal example involves my running. When I first started, I had a certain course that I followed each day. And, at the time, it took me about 30 minutes each day to complete it. Well, I have always been well aware that I am not training for the Olympics. Rather than continue along the same old path day after day, I decided I could run anywhere—as long as I ran for 30 minutes. I realized that would accomplish the same exercise, but that I would have more variety.

Now, I know that for some people they want to run a certain distance or try to push themselves to a particular pace. But for me, I just wanted to do something that would be good for me. So, rather than worry about whether it was 2.8 miles or 3.3 miles, I made a deal with myself that if I just jog in any direction for 30 minutes, then I would be happy. Although I now run farther distances, I still only gauge them by time. In other words, if I decide that my pace is about 9 minutes per mile, then if I want to run seven miles I judge it by running 63 minutes. This way I can head in any direction that I want and it provides a much greater variety in my exercise.

This same approach can apply in almost anything you do, but it is particularly effective in biking, walking, or running. You can go wherever you want and not be worried about exactly how far or fast you went. If taking this approach allows you to maintain interest more, then give it a try and don't feel guilty at all!

A time limit can also be used as a maximum to help enable you to establish positive exercise habits. For me, I always feel as if I should be doing more. So, for example, when I started lifting weights, I would go from 30 minutes to 45 to an hour, and continue to raise the amount of time I would lift. I also realized that if I continued at that pace, eventually I would be more likely to quit altogether. By setting a maximum of 45 minutes—and when I get to that point I automatically stop for the day—it allows me to have a higher intensity and prevents me from burning out.

Being aware of what works best for you can allow you to sustain or even increase a program that fits your lifestyle and needs. If self-imposed time minimums or maximums work well for you, then use them to assist in providing the structure needed to make exercise a lifelong part of your being.

4

WHAT'S THE BIG DEAL ABOUT FITNESS?

If you are only looking at this book because you are in a panic trying to fit into that bathing suit that you are going to wear on your vacation in two weeks you might be tempted to skip this section. Before you make that decision let me ask you two questions. Has anyone in your immediate family been diagnosed with heart disease or had a heart attack? Has anyone in your immediate family suffered from cancer?

These two questions tend to shift our perspectives regarding the importance of physical fitness. Each semester I ask my undergraduate students to raise their hands if a parent or grandparent has had a heart attack or been diagnosed with heart disease. The first year I asked this question I was shocked at the response. In a group of 120 students, nearly 80 hands raised in response to my question. That's two-thirds of the class. I then asked how many had parents or grandparents that had been diagnosed with cancer of any sort. Again, the response was overwhelming. Unfortunately, the number of students raising their hands over time has not diminished, rather it has increased.

The three leading killers in our society, heart disease, cancer, and stroke, can be greatly reduced by improving our physical fitness levels. Countless studies have shown this fact to be true, yet as a society we are still not exercising. Sixty percent of American adults don't get the recommended amount of exercise and 25 percent don't exercise at all. My question is, *why not?*

I have a few ideas about why people don't exercise. Some of these ideas come from responses of my students and some are my own reflections about people in general. I believe that it is fair to assume that most of the population knows of the health risks that accompany not exercising. However, knowing a fact and understanding relationship between fact and ourselves are different things. We tend to think of ourselves separately from facts that we know are true for people in general. All of us in some way suffer from the "it won't happen to me" syndrome. The trick in breaking this habit is to make a personal connection with it. Let me give you an example from my life.

I know what the experts say regarding the benefits of exercise. I'm one of those experts. I have taught the statistics and I have warned students about the "evils" of not exercising; but I did it thinking it was "them" who needed to know this information. I teach physical fitness for a living and therefore I must be immune. I didn't realize it at the time, but I was doing my students and myself a disservice. I was teaching fact with no personal commitment. I have found that teaching something that you are passionate about is much easier than teaching something you are merely interested in. It took a call in April of 1996 that completely changed my perspective. I remember waking up to a call from my mother on a chilly Tuesday morning. Mom had been diagnosed with breast cancer. As I tried to gather my thoughts to offer some encouraging words, she proceeded to tell me that the cancer was very advanced and that the tumor was large and had spread to her lymph nodes. Not only could I not offer encouragement, I was unable to breathe. I felt as if I had been punched in the stomach. The following days passed in a blur but I distinctly remember a conversation my father had with the oncologist. "Will she be all right?" asked my father. The reply from the doctor was, "Start enjoying every day."

Now, I had a personal connection. There was two ways I could think of to help my mother. One was to support her with love, and the other was to get her exercising. Today my mother and I take as many walks together as we can. It's been almost five years since that cold April morning and my mother is still enjoying every day. And, so am I. Although there is no specific research about the effect of walking in regards to my mother's illness, I firmly believe that exercise has played a significant role in her battle with cancer.

I hope her story will give you a glimpse into the nondis-criminatory world of chronic diseases. We are all vulnerable, but our vulnerability can be lessened through regular partici-pation in exercise. We are responsible for our health and hap-piness. We must learn to be proactive in regard to chronic dis-eases. Lessening our chances for developing heart disease, cancer, and stroke are only part of the power of exercise. Regu-lar exercise has been linked to improved self-esteem, greater energy levels, weight control, improved stress management, and a slowing of the aging process. All of these benefits help us enjoy life more fully.

Fitness is a big deal, and to a large degree we are in the driver's seat to a happy and healthy life. Once we realize the extent that exercise can have on our quality of life we can more easily develop a personal connection to it. Elinor Smith once wrote, "It had long since come to my attention that people of accomplishment rarely sat back and let things happen to them. They went out and happened to things." Educators gen-erally are goal driven people. You give your heart and soul to your work, sometimes at the expense of your physical well-be-ing. The world needs dedicated educators, so take a little time for some self-care so you can continue to make a difference in your student's lives. I hope my mother's story has empowered you to believe that you can make a difference in your health by exercising. I know how much her illness and recovery have impacted my beliefs and behaviors.

5

BUT I DON'T LIKE TO SWEAT...

For most educators, the thought of returning form a noontime walk drenched in sweat is not a pleasant image. No one feels comfortable perspiring in dress clothes, particularly when their schedule doesn't provide adequate time to freshen up before returning to classes. For years I have heard people in all professions complain about how they dislike sweating. I usually ask them if it is the actual process of sweating that they dislike or the fact that they must then take time out of their busy schedule to get cleaned up again. Most of the time people admit that it isn't the sweating that is so bothersome; rather it is the amount of time that is lost in the locker room. Educators value time. At secondary schools, your day is broken into a series of 50-minute periods with two- to five-minute intervals of movement between classrooms. At the elementary level, it may even be more restrictive. It is understandable why time management issues weigh so heavily in decisions of what to do and what not to do.

One of the greatest aspects of exercise is that you don't have to perspire to reap its benefits. A healthy lifestyle is a personal journey that is made up of steps of various lengths and paces. Once you make the decision to lead a healthy life, your journey has begun. Like all journeys, you will have periods where you feel that your progress is slow. Those are times when you must remember that any step is better than no step because every time we do some kind of movement or exercise we are getting a little bit closer to a better, healthier life.

It is also important that we learn to pace our journey. There are times in our lives that aren't conducive to sweat-inducing levels of intensity. If you aren't feeling well one day, take the day off. Don't exercise when you are physically ill. Remember to pace, not race. The same idea applies when you are at work in your professional clothes. If you don't want to perspire at work, then only do exercises that can be done without breaking a sweat. Don't let the fact you do not want to sweat stop you from doing a few little exercises. Every movement or exercise that you do helps to burn calories, and any weight bearing movement helps to improve bone density and prevent muscle atrophy.

A journey of health and wellness is centered on striking balances in your life: between work and play, career and family, self-care and care for others, mental and physical stimulation, and high intensity and low intensity activities. Too much of any variable can cause burnout and too little of any variable can cause rust-out. The challenge is to find an acceptable balance, one that is not too challenging or demanding and one that is challenging enough to allow for physical and mental growth.

Let's look at the variable of exercise in this context. If your exercise regime is too physically taxing, your body's immune system will begin to break down and you could get ill. If, on the other hand, your routine is not taxing at all you will not get the potential benefits that a more vigorous program would offer. Exercise programs that are not challenging tend to become boring and monotonous. It is difficult to stay with something that is not in the least bit challenging—especially for an overachieving educator!

One simple way of striking a balance between moderate-intensity and low-intensity exercise is to use perspiration as a workout gauge. Use low-intensity exercises (exercises that don't induce sweating) when you are at work or at times when you don't have immediate access to shower facilities. Use moderate-intensity exercises (exercises that induce sweating) when you have access to shower facilities.

In controlled environments, such as buildings, and in moderate outdoor temperatures, sweating is often a good indicator of exercise intensity. The body produces perspiration as a means of temperature control during activities that raise the body's internal heat. The higher the intensity the more you sweat. It is not the perspiration, however, that actually cools the body. It is the evaporation of the perspiration that cools the body. Understanding the role of perspiration in exercise intensity provides you with a gauge to measure that intensity so you can strike a balance between low-intensity and moderate-intensity exercise.

If returning to classes after a noontime walk, drenched in perspiration is not appealing to you, don't sweat it! Just walk slower or not as far. You are still doing your health a favor.

PART III

TAKING CONTROL

6

IF IT WASN'T GOOD ENOUGH, IT WOULDN'T BE THE MINIMUM—SETTING REALISTIC GOALS

Sometimes deciding how to get to an endpoint is as much or more of a challenge than determining what that endpoint is. Establishing reasonable and personalized long- and short-term goals can help us accomplish what we want in the areas of weight loss and fitness.

There is the story of an elderly man and woman driving endlessly out in the middle of no where. After much deliberation, the woman turns to the man and asks, "Do you know where you are going?" And he replies, "No, but I am making great time."

If we don't establish appropriate ways to get there, whatever "get there" means to you, we may not even know when we have. And, if we do not develop short-term goals, then we may be much more likely to get discouraged at what we perceive as a lack of progress. If in our mind we would like to lose 35 pounds and after four weeks have lost 6, we can perceive that as a positive or a negative. Establishing realistic checkpoints along the way may allow us to reach our destination in a more appropriate manner.

PERSONALIZE YOUR GOALS

One of the things we attempt to do in this book is to not provide a cookie-cutter approach to fitness. Instead, we are well aware that everyone is at a different point and that different things will work for different people. This is why it is so essential that you determine an approach that works for you.

We read a lot of articles in a multitude of magazines that talk about miracle diets or the latest weight-loss fad. And though we hear many negative things about most of them, we still hear of, or even know personally, people that for some reason found something that actually worked for them. Though someone may refer to some strategy as a silly idea, if it works for you, then there is no way it is silly. Developing a personal approach is a key to making something stick for each individual.

In Chapter 7, we discuss scheduling time to work out. For some people this can be tremendously beneficial; for others, it could be totally ineffective. Maybe walking two miles has appeal to you, but maybe making it a 30-minute timed walk would be better. In this chapter, we will provide methods that you can use that will provide some structure and a sense of accountability. These may make it easier for you to stick to the course. We also want to help you establish an understanding of what is a *realistic goal* and determine methods which can assist your ability to monitor yourself as you are making progress.

WRITE IT DOWN

For some people, everything that they write down, they do. Some of us live by lists. And for others, the only thing we do with lists are throw them away when we don't do them. None of these are inherently right or wrong, but finding something that works best for you is critical. If having a monthly calendar on which you prescribe your goals for daily exercise and even diet in advance works for you, then by all means do it.

By the same token, if reflecting after the fact gives you a feeling of satisfaction, then document when you are done what you have accomplished. I am not someone who likes to think much in advance about what I will do in terms of working out, but for several years I would write down how far I ran each day. Then, at the end of the year I could total up the miles, count the number of days missed, and so on. I never did much with the information, but it was fun for me to do.

If any of these strategies works for you, then you should use them to your advantage. A good friend of mine who is a very dedicated exerciser likes to map out his week each Monday. He finds that this allows him to set short-term goals that he is planning to meet. It also allows him to plan in his rest days. He feels that this is the motivation he needs to get through days when he is less than fired up about exercise. For him seeing that he will take Thursday off, for example, is a big incentive for him to do what he has planned for the remainder of the days in a week.

A simpler logging approach is to just use a few words in a logbook. Whether you are goal setting or record keeping, you could write down something simple like "walk, 20 minutes"; "lift weights, 15 minutes"; and so on. This can give you a general sense of what you either did or are aiming to do without the paperwork being restrictive. You could even combine your regular lesson plan book with your exercise log. Next to "Tuesday—math test," you could write "Tuesday—treadmill 3 miles." You have to decide if that is more or less stressful for you, but it is a way to combine your professional responsibilities with meeting your personal needs. Obviously, you could also keep track of your daily goals and then record in a different color what you actually did. This might be a nice incentive to help start and continue a regular fitness routine.

These same ideas can apply to working on your diet. Either in planning or after the fact, you can log how your eating is going. Maybe it can be general terms like did well, or not so good. You could even use a 1-to-5 or a 1-to-10 scale and see if you have any patterns. Maybe each Sunday night you load up because the weekend is over or Tuesday is pizza day at school. This is not meant to prevent you from ever straying in your eating. There is nothing at all wrong with splurging at times. However, this approach may help you curb a little each week, which can eventually make tremendous rewards.

If seeing goals written down moves you into actually doing something, then sharpen your pencil. However, if not meeting those goals turns you toward the cookie jar, then let that instead be a guide to help you meet your needs. Some of us do what ever we have written in our plan books or calendars. Others view planning only as a distraction from the time we could be exercising. Developing a method that works best for you is an important part of planning and improving your health.

7

FINDING THE TIME
AND THE ENERGY

We often think that one of the biggest obstacles we face is to "find the time" to take care of ourselves. There is no shortage of seminars that teach time management. And, though, we all would like to have more hours in the day, finding the time to do something for ourselves is one factor that we all face. However, an equally challenging snag is often trying to find the energy. This chapter looks at how we can find the time and the energy to keep moving toward our exercise and health goals. Being able to manage ourselves is a critical part of being able to improve our physical self.

WE ALWAYS FIND TIME FOR WHAT IS MOST IMPORTANT

Though we all feel that we do not have enough "extra" time to focus on taking care of ourselves, we do somehow find the time to gripe, whine, or complain about not having the time! We really do have enough time to do what is most important, we just have to decide that taking care of ourselves needs to be higher up on that list.

Stephen Covey (*The 7 habits of highly effective people*. New York: Simon & Schuster, 1989) talks about doing what is important over doing what is urgent. It is amazing, but somehow we make ourselves feel that so many things in life are urgent. However, effective people, somehow or another, even with all of the things that seem urgent, still make sure that they have time for what is important.

Another irony in all of this is that once we get into a regular routine of exercising and taking care of ourselves, we often realize that many of the things that seemed so urgent really aren't that urgent at all. Thus, by committing the time to exercise, we may actually gain more time in our lives. This could be because with a boost in energy we can be more efficient and effective. Or, it might be because things that seemed so critical before soon melt away.

I mentioned earlier that if I went out running in the morning, then dealing with an upset parent did not seem like such a big deal after all. Though I approached the situation with the same level of concern and sensitivity, the sense of calm that I felt was very refreshing and reinforcing. Our ability to have a more appropriate and positive perspective is essential in order for us to take care of ourselves and be the true professionals that we need to be as educators.

With so much publicity being critical of educators in newspapers and on radio call-in shows, we have to make sure that we have the strength to continue to do what we know is right, even in the most challenging of times. Actually, we need more determination and inner resolve to do that now than ever. And, luckily it is up to us to find the right way. It is not up to anyone else. If we had to rely on others to take care of us, we had sure better hope that our caregiver has the energy to take care of at least two people—and one of them is you!

SCHEDULE TIME FOR YOURSELF

If you are someone that somehow does whatever is in your personal calendar or lesson plan book, then make sure that exercise gets scheduled also. When I was a principal in my first year, I struggled finding the time to visit and observe in classrooms on a daily or even regular basis. No matter how hard I tried, something else "more important" always seemed to come up. The only solution that I could ever get to work for me was to write in 15- or 20-minute times each day in my calendar book. That way, when the time arrived, I just did it because it was written in. It is amazing, but if someone got my calendar book and wrote "Jump off a cliff at 3:30," I think I would be looking for that cliff at 3:20 because it was written down in my calendar!

You may not be quite that time driven, but scheduling time for ourselves and our exercise program can be very helpful in our efforts to make exercise a regular part of our life. One thing that I have done for years is to get up at 5:15 in the morning and either run or lift weights. I can hear some of you saying, "But, I'm not a morning person!" Well, I wasn't either, but I promise you a few months of getting up at 5:15 to exercise and you will be! This is so especially when you can start your day with such a positive attitude and feeling.

For me that early morning schedule was so helpful because it did not take away time from my family or work. I would typically get back from my run or home from the gym at about the same time I would have been getting up. The only difference was instead of staggering out of bed at 6:15, I was energized and ready to face the day with a vigor that I never had under other circumstances. And, since exercise often assists you in sleeping better, I actually have felt more refreshed since getting into that routine. And, I did not feel guilty because I was not taking away from my job, wife, or family. Instead, I was contributing much more to them—and to myself.

The most positive benefit in making sure you find the time needed to take care of yourself physically is that amazingly, that helps you discover the energy you need also.

FINDING THE ENERGY

Though most of us feel that taking control of our time is one of the biggest obstacles to exercising more regularly, I actually believe that finding the energy needed is more of a preventer.

It is amazing when you think about it, but reflect back to a time that you felt great about yourself. Think of the frame of mind you had, how you felt that no mountain was too steep to climb and that almost literally you could accomplish anything that you wanted to. Just imagine the amount of things you can get done in just an hour when you feel like that. When you are energized, motivated, and excited about life and what you are doing, there are no limits to your potential. You can accomplish more in 60 minutes when you feel like that than you can in a typical entire day. Well, that is the point.

Conversely, think how hard it is to accomplish anything when you feel sorry for yourself, or feel down in the dumps. Not only do challenging tasks seem great, but even simple tasks may also seem impossible. When you feel charged up and excited, you can readily fly through stacks of papers to grade, or tasks to do. However, when you are zapped, just stapling two sheets of paper together can almost seem insurmountable.

With this in mind, if you could set aside a few minutes so that you could feel energized the rest of your day, wouldn't that actually make you more effective and, in the long run, *save* you time! Wow, just think how nice it would be to set aside the time needed to exercise and take care of yourself and yet have more energy to be more productive and feel better for the rest of the day. That is exactly what can happen when you do find the time to exercise.

When you find the time to exercise, you soon discover the energy to do all of the other tasks that you need to do. And, if you can approach your routine daily activities with a renewed energy and vigor, you most likely will actually find yourself having more time than ever before. Just imagine, finding the time to do something positive for yourself can give you the energy to more effectively take care of your families, and all of the students that are in your classes, schools, and universities.

TIME IS PRECIOUS

We know that all busy educators have a limited amount of time. In order to accommodate this intense and very busy lifestyle, there are special tricks and approaches that can be done that will allow you to fit exercise and fitness into your already too full lives.

One thing that can be done is to not be afraid to let yourself off the hook. Always be aware that anything is better than nothing and though you might want to get in a 40-minute workout, maybe today, 20 is all that you have. Rather than disgustedly dropping that 20-minute possibility down to nothing, take advantage of whatever opportunities you have. For years, I tried to set aside an hour to work out every morning. As I mentioned earlier, I would typically wake up at 5:15 each morning. If I had an early meeting, I would get up even earlier so that I could get my full hour in.

Once I finally let myself do less when it was more appropriate, it let me be much more practical in my approach. It also kept me doing *something* every day. If I only had 20 minutes several years ago I would do nothing at all, or even worse, sulk over a couple of donuts. Now, I would take advantage of whatever window of opportunity I had and realize it is so much better doing anything than doing nothing at all or, worse yet, doing something else I would be unhappy about later.

Knowing how important your time is, Chapter 8 outlines some of the things that we can do in short chunks of time that we may be able to free up before or after work, squeeze in during the day, or even manage while making our commute in the car. Even if our goal is to commit 30 minutes a day to exercise, there may be a way to do that in three 10-minute allotments, especially if that is all that our busy day allows.

Finding time to take care of ourselves can help each of us more effectively take care of our time.

8

THE 10-MINUTE WORKOUT—THE LITTLE THINGS ADD UP

A humorous, but oh-so-true definition of a teacher is someone who can drink three cups of coffee before 8:00 AM and hold it until 3:30 PM. Most of us don't have the luxury of an hour or two of free time during the day that we can run to the gym for a workout. Being able to be creative and to fit our fitness into 10-minute increments can allow all of us to make exercise part of our daily schedule. It simply takes a little creative planning and we will be on our way in making a difference in our long-term fitness and weight management goals.

How many times during your daily schedule do you find yourself with just enough time to worry about what you need to get done but not enough time to even get started doing it? A friend once told me that if you want to be successful at anything in life you must not wait for the big breaks or the uninterrupted blocks of time to accomplish things. You must learn to use small increments of time during your day efficiently. This skill must be learned. If you don't plan for these little "breaks in your day" it will be too late to make use of them. You must be prepared and you must be consistent. It is these small increments of time that add up to help make large changes in your life.

The following are some ideas that might help you make use of those wonderful bits of free time during your day. Remember, the little things, done over time, add up!

AT THE WHEEL WORKOUT

There are several things that you can do while driving that are beneficial to your health and well-being. The following exercises are used primarily for calorie burning, muscle toning, and stress relief.

1. *Steering Wheel Squeezes:* While sitting at a red light, grip the steering wheel at 10 o'clock and 2 o'clock (remember, safety first!) and squeeze and release for 10 repetitions. This exercise works both the forearms and the biceps, provided you do it with your elbows slightly bent (Figure 8.1).

FIGURE 8.1. STEERING WHEEL SQUEEZES

2. *Abdominal Crunches:* Execute sets of 25 abdominal crunches while you drive or ride in the car. Tilt your hips slightly forward and exhale as you bend forward squeezing your abs (Figure 8.2).

FIGURE 8.2. ABDOMINAL CRUNCHES

These crunches are identical to those you do lying flat. The only change is the angle in which you perform them. Don't worry about looking silly while doing this exercise. People watching you from other cars will think you are listening to a song that has a good, even beat!

3. *Curls and Lifts:* The next time you are stuck at a railroad crossing, try this exercise. Put the car in park and place both of your hands on your car seat keeping your arms close to your hips. Press down into the seat and attempt to lift your body slightly off the seat (Figure 8.3).

FIGURE 8.3. LIFT

It doesn't matter whether you can lift your body into the air. The important part of this technique is that you get your arms fully extended and you squeeze your triceps in an extended position for two to four seconds. Immediately follow this exercise with a biceps curl. Keep your elbows at your side and move both hands toward your shoulders (Figure 8.4). Squeeze your biceps for two to four seconds in this position. Repeat these two exercises in succession until the train has passed or you unable to lift your arms back up to the steering wheel.

FIGURE 8.4. CURL

4. Racquetball Squeeze: A variation to the steering wheel squeeze is to use a racquetball. This exercise allows you to work one arm at a time while you drive (Figure 8.5). The racquetball is more versatile than the steering wheel also. You can execute squeezes while you curl your hand toward your shoulder to work the biceps in conjunction with the forearm or try extending your arm as you do these squeezes. In addition, this variation will work your triceps.

FIGURE 8.5 RACQUETBALL SQUEEZE

Try these exercises and you will find that a 10-minute drive can be an invigorating experience. You may even begin to look forward to those stoplights and long trains. Besides, now you will be warmed up for the next phase of your training...the parking lot power walk!

PARKING LOT POWER WALK

Be honest! How many times have you driven around the parking lot looking for the closest open space? I know people who will drive around and around a parking lot hunting for a close space to park. This searching can go on for 10 minutes! If you are serious about losing weight and feeling better; then the parking lot problem is your solution. If you are lucky enough to find a full parking lot, rejoice! You have just driven into another opportunity to become more healthy. Parking 100 yards away from your building every day will greatly increase your caloric expenditure. If your parking lot isn't huge, park at the furthest point and zigzag up and down the aisles to make your walk as long as possible.

Afraid people will think you are crazy for wandering aimlessly around the parking lot? The solution is to bring lots of stuff to school each day. Keep several bags, boxes, and books in your back seat or trunk to be used as decoys to disguise your real mission, which is to make several trips in and out of the building! Not only will your colleagues think that you are a dedicated and highly creative teacher—why else would she be carrying all those bags of teaching aids?—but you will get an even greater workout by carrying these bags while you walk. Don't believe that it will make a difference whether or not you carry a bag or two into the building? Try this experiment sometime, perhaps even with your class. Walk at a normal pace for 30 seconds without carrying anything. Take your pulse when you have completed the time interval. Now, do the same 30-second walk, but this time carry a full bookbag. Take your pulse at the end of the 30 seconds. An elevated heart rate means that you have increased your workout intensity. Higher intensity means more calories burned and greater benefit for your heart. Now get out to the parking lot and bring in those teaching aids. Plus, however far away you park, you double the benefit when you walk back to the car at the end of the day!

DON'T JUST STAND THERE...
TAKE THE STAIRS

Have you ever wondered why every health club around the country has stair machines? The reason they spend thousands of dollars for these machines is because climbing (or descending) stairs burns calories and tones leg muscles. Most people know the benefits of taking the stairs and yet they never do. Why? They don't want to sweat? How many educators other than those in higher education work in building that are more than three floors? If sweating is an issue then walk one or two flights of stairs. You don't have to run up or down the stairs. It's not a race, it's a way of life. If you do work in a building with several floors, take the elevator to the second or third floor, then get off and walk the last couple flights of stairs.

Many people complain that taking the stairs hurts their knees. This is a legitimate concern. Walking stairs does put more stress on the knees than walking on level ground. If your knees bother you on stairs, something you might want to consider is that walking up stairs is much less stressful on the knees than walking down. If possible, take the stairs up and ride the elevator down.

The important thing to remember is that these little things do add up over time. The trick is to make a commitment to yourself to take the stairs before you are standing in front of the elevator trying to decide if you should take the stairs. Just do it!

The DYNAMIC OFFICE

There is not a classroom or office that cannot be transformed into your personal workout area. All it takes is a little creativity. If your working area has a doorway, at least one wall, a desk and a chair, you are in business. Ten minutes is all it takes to get a fantastic workout. Give these exercises a try the next time you have a few minutes open up in your work day.

1. *Wall Push-Ups:* This is not as difficult as it sounds. Stand about two feet from a wall in your workspace. Make sure this is a support wall and not a temporary divider. Reach out to the wall and place you palms on the wall at shoulder height and slightly wider than shoulder width (Figure 8.6).

FIGURE 8.6. WALL PUSH-UP—GETTING READY

Keeping your knees slightly bent, bend your arms so your torso is brought closer to the wall (Figure 8.7). Once you have almost touched the

FIGURE 8.7. WALL PUSH-UP—ARMS BENT

wall with your forehead, push your body away until you are once again at extended arm length. This movement should resemble a push-up, only it is done vertically. As you become stronger at this exercise, you can make it more difficult by moving your feet further away from the wall. You can also change the positioning of your hands to change the major muscle group being stressed. For instance, the closer your hands are to your torso, the more you are working your triceps. The further your hands are from your torso, the more you are working your chest.

2. *Chair Push-Ups:* This exercise is much more difficult than the previous one. Place two sturdy chairs facing one another with just enough space between them to fit your torso. As you face the chairs, place your left hand on the seat of the left chair and your right hand on the seat of the right chair. Your feet should be behind you enough to make your body resemble a straight line. This position should look like a normal push up, only on an angle (Figure 8.8). Lower your body until your

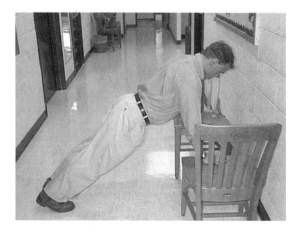

FIGURE 8.8. CHAIR PUSH-UP—GETTING READY

shoulders are slightly below your elbows (Figure 8.9). Raise your torso back up to the starting position where your arms are fully extended. Make sure to go through the range of motion in a controlled manner.

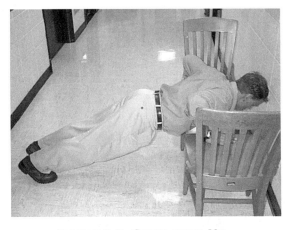

**FIGURE 8.9. CHAIR PUSH-UP—
SHOULDERS SLIGHTLY BELOW ELBOWS**

3. *Chair Dips:* If the back part of your arms are not as tight as you would like, then this exercise is for you! Begin by sitting on the edge of a chair. Grip the front edge of the chair on each side of your legs. Slide your hips off the chair by walking your feet out in front of you (Figure 8.10). Keep your knees bent at 90 degrees and lower your hips toward the floor (Figure 8.11). Once you reach a 90-degree angle with your elbows, raise your hips back up until your arms are fully extended. Try to keep your elbows facing toward the back of the chair as you execute this movement. This exercise will really tone your triceps.

FIGURE 8.10. CHAIR DIP—GETTING READY

FIGURE 8.11. CHAIR DIP—HIPS LOWERED

4. *Desk Squats:* Place one hand on your desk to aid in supporting your weight during this exercise (Figure 8.12). With your feet shoulder-width apart,

FIGURE 8.12. DESK SQUAT—GETTING READY

slowly lower your body by bending your knees. Stop your descent when your upper legs are parallel to the floor (Figure 8.13). Remember to keep your torso upright as you lower and raise your body. As you become stronger at this exercise, try executing it without using the support of the desk. A more advanced version of this exercise can be done while holding books to add more resistance (Figure 8.14).

**FIGURE 8.13. DESK SQUAT—
LEGS PARALLEL TO FLOOR**

**FIGURE 8.14. DESK SQUAT—
WITH ADDED WEIGHT**

5. *Shoulder Raises:* Begin this exercise with your
    arms at your side. Hold a book in each hand that
    is of equal weight (Figure 8.15). Raise your arms

FIGURE 8.15. SHOULDER RAISE—GETTING READY

in front of your body to shoulder height and
lower them back down to your side in a controlled manner (Figure 8.16). Immediately follow
this exercise by raising your arms out from your
sides to a T-position and then lower your arms
back down to your side (Figure 8.17). This exercise works the front and side of your shoulders.

**FIGURE 8.16. SHOULDER RAISE—
RAISE TO THE FRONT**

FIGURE 8.17. SHOULDER RAISE—RAISE TO THE SIDE

6. *Shoulder Shrugs:* This exercise begins with your arms at your side (Figure 8.18). While holding a

FIGURE 8.18. SHOULDER SHRUG—GETTING READY

book of equal weight in each hand, lift your shoulders directly up toward the ceiling. Imagine trying to touch your ears with your shoulders while doing this exercise (Figure 8.19). Make sure to squeeze your trapezius muscles (the muscles connecting your neck with your shoulders) at the top of this exercise before you relax and lower your shoulders. Try repeating this exercise for 10 repetitions. You can increase the difficulty by adding more or heavier books.

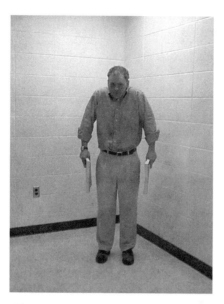

FIGURE 8.19. SHOULDER SHRUG

7. *Calf Raises:* Place your hands flat against a wall at shoulder height (Figure 8.20). Shift all of your

FIGURE 8.20. CALF RAISE—GETTING READY

body weight to the balls of your feet and raise your heels off the ground (Figure 8.21). Repeat

FIGURE 8.21. CALF RAISE—LIFT OFF!

this exercise for 15 repetitions. As you become better at this exercise, place an old book under your feet to increase the range of motion that you can go through while doing this exercise (Figure 8.22).

FIGURE 8.22. CALF RAISE—
INCREASING RANGE OF MOTION

8. *Chair Crunches:* This exercise works your abdominal muscles while you sit in a chair (Figure 8.23).

FIGURE 8.23. CHAIR CRUNCH—GETTING READY

Tilt your hips slightly forward and exhale as you
bend forward (Figure 8.24). These crunches are
identical to those you do lying flat. Try to work
up to four sets of 25 repetitions.

**FIGURE 8.24. CHAIR CRUNCH—
EXHALE WHILE BENDING**

9. *Floor Crunches:* To really work those abdominals, lie on your back with your knees bent and your feet flat on the floor (Figure 8.25). Pick a spot on

FIGURE 8.25. FLOOR CRUNCH—GETTING READY

the ceiling and remain looking at it as you slowly exhale and raise your head and shoulders slightly off the floor by squeezing your abdominal muscles (Figure 8.26). Relax your stomach muscles

**FIGURE 8.26. FLOOR CRUNCH—
HEAD AND SHOULDERS SLIGHTLY OFF THE FLOOR**

and lower your shoulders back to the ground in a slow and controlled manner. Try to work up to four sets of 25 repetitions.

10. *Arm Curls:* This exercise tones and strengthens the biceps, the muscle in the front of your upper arm. Start this exercise with your feet shoulder-width distance apart and your knees slightly bent for stabilization. Hold a stapler or some other object in your hand with your arm resting extended at your side (Figure 8.27). Keep your elbow close

FIGURE 8.27. ARM CURL—GETTING READY

to your side as you squeeze your biceps to raise your hand to shoulder height (Figure 8.28). Lower your hand back to your side in a slow and controlled manner. Try to work up to 12 repetitions of this movement.

FIGURE 8.28. ARM CURL—
ALMOST ANYTHING CAN BE A WEIGHT

FORGET THE HOME GYM— USE YOUR HOME AS A GYM

Most people don't realize the extent of what our homes offer in the realm of exercise opportunities. Many exercises can be done in the privacy of your home without spending hundreds or thousands of dollars on home exercise equipment. The following exercises can be done quickly and easily. And, if you do some of each, you will hit all of the major muscle groups.

1. *Standing Kickback*: This exercise works the glutes (your rear end), lower back, and hamstrings. Stand with your feet shoulder-width apart. Raise your left arm up in front of you to shoulder height

as you extend your right leg back behind you as far as you can (Figure 8.29). To make this exercise really effective you must concentrate on keeping your glutes flexed. Do 10 to 15 repetitions on each side.

FIGURE 8.29. STANDING KICKBACK

2. *Arm Curls:* Grab a can of soup or a gallon of milk and try this exercise that works the front part of the arm called the biceps. Start this exercise with your feet shoulder-width distance apart and your knees slightly bent for stabilization. Hold the weighted object in your hand with your arm resting extended at your side (Figure 8.30). Keep your elbow close to your side as you squeeze your biceps to raise your hand to shoulder height (Figure 8.31). Be sure to execute this movement in a controlled manner. Try to work up to 12 repetitions of this movement.

FIGURE 8.30. ARM CURL—GETTING READY

**FIGURE 8.31. ARM CURL—ELBOWS IN,
RAISE ARMS TO SHOULDER HEIGHT**

3. *Triceps Kickbacks:* Place your left knee on the seat
    of a chair or on some stable object in your home.
    With a can of soup in your right hand, lean for-
    ward and place your left hand on the object your
    knee is resting upon. Keep your right elbow close
    to your side with your triceps parallel to the floor
    and your right hand pointing straight down (Fig-
    ure 8.32). Extend your right arm so your hand

**FIGURE 8.32. TRICEPS KICKBACK—
GETTING IN POSITION**

moves in a backward direction until your entire
arm is extended and parallel to the floor (Figure
8.33). Squeeze the triceps in this extended position and then slowly lower the weight back to the
starting position. Try to work up to 12 repetitions
on each arm.

FIGURE 8.33. TRICEPS KICKBACK—ARM EXTENDED

4. *Lunges:* Begin this exercise by standing with your feet together and your hands on your hips (Figure 8.34). Take an extended step forward with your right leg. Your step should be long enough to cause your left heel to raise from the ground. From this extended position, lower your body toward the ground in a controlled manner. Your left knee should not touch the ground in the lowered position and your right knee should not travel past your toes (Figure 8.35). Push backwards with your right heel and step your right leg back to its original position. Use small steps when you first begin doing this exercise until you are comfortable with the movement and you have developed the strength needed to do a full lunge. Try to work up to 12 repetitions on each leg. This exercise works the quadriceps and hamstrings.

FIGURE 8.34. LUNGE—GETTING READY

**FIGURE 8.35. LUNGE—A FULL LUNGE
WITH KNEE JUST OFF THE FLOOR**

5. *Wall Push-Up:* As mentioned in the section on the dynamic office, this is not as difficult as it sounds. Stand about two feet from a wall in your living space. Reach out to the wall and place your palms on the wall at shoulder height and slightly wider than shoulder width (Figure 8.36). Keeping your

FIGURE 8.36. WALL PUSH-UP—GETTING READY

knees slightly bent, bend your arms so your torso is brought closer to the wall (Figure 8.37). Once you have almost touched the wall with your forehead, push your body away until you are once again at extended arm's length. This movement should resemble a push-up, only it is done vertically. As you become stronger at this exercise, you can make it more difficult by moving your feet further away from the wall. You can also change the positioning of your hands to change the major muscle group being stressed. For instance, the closer your hands are to your torso, the more you are working your triceps. The further your hands are from your torso, the more you are working your chest.

FIGURE 8.37. WALL PUSH-UP

6. *One-Arm Row:* Place your left knee on the seat of a chair or on some stable object in your home. With a can of soup or a gallon of milk in your right hand, lean forward and place your left hand on the object your knee is resting upon. Let your right arm hang straight down toward the floor (Figure 8.38). Pull the object in your hand straight up toward your hip. Imagine putting something in your back pocket. Keep your elbow close to your side and try to keep your back flat and parallel to the floor during this exercise (Figure 8.39). Squeeze your back at the top of this movement for two seconds and then lower the object in a controlled manner. Try to work up to 12 repetitions on each arm. This exercise will work the middle back.

FIGURE 8.38. ONE-ARM ROW—GETTING IN POSITION

FIGURE 8.39. ONE-ARM ROW—KEEP THE BACK FLAT

7. *Shoulder Raises:* Begin this exercise with your arms at your side. Hold a can of soup in each hand that is of equal weight (Figure 8.40). Raise your arms in front of your body to shoulder height and lower them back down to your side in a controlled manner (Figure 8.41). Immediately follow this exercise by raising your arms out from your sides to a T-position and then lower your arms back down to your side (Figure 8.42). This exercise works the front and side of your deltoids (shoulders).

FIGURE 8.40. SHOULDER RAISES—GETTING READY

FIGURE 8.41. SHOULDER RAISES—TO THE FRONT

**FIGURE 8.42. SHOULDER RAISES—
TO THE SIDE**

8. *Calf Raises:* Place your hands flat against a wall at
    shoulder height (Figure 8.43). Shift all of your
    body weight to the balls of your feet and raise
    your heels off the ground (Figure 8.44). Repeat
    this exercise for 15 repetitions. As you become
    better at this exercise, place an old book under
    your feet to increase the range of motion that you
    can go through while doing this exercise.

FIGURE 8.43. CALF RAISES—GETTING READY

FIGURE 8.44. CALF RAISES—
RAISE YOUR HEELS

9. *Floor Crunches:* To really work those abdominal muscles, lie on your back with your knees bent and your feet flat on the floor. Pick a spot on the ceiling and remain looking at it as you slowly exhale and raise your head and shoulders slightly off the floor by squeezing your abdominal muscles (Figure 8.45). Relax your stomach muscles and lower your shoulders back to the ground in a slow and controlled manner. Try to work up to four sets of 25 repetitions.

**FIGURE 8.45 FLOOR CRUNCHES—
HEAD AND SHOULDERS SLIGHTLY OFF THE FLOOR**

As you can see, whether at work, home, or in between, we can always squeeze in a little time for some fitness fun. By combining little windows of opportunity for exercise, we can open doors to a better life.

9
KEEPING IT UP
THROUGH THE SUMMER

Summer has arrived! For most educators, this is a time of relaxing, regrouping, and recuperating. After nine months of giving your very best to every student, you deserve a break. It's a perfect time for a little more self-care. Catch up on some pleasure reading, travel to new or familiar destinations, see a movie, and stay on that exercise program that you started during the school year.

As an educator, you understand the importance of evaluating what actions are beneficial in reaching your teaching goals. It is equally important that you take some time to evaluate how well you fared on reaching your personal fitness goals. Summer provides an opportunity to do so. Did you have your 10-minute workout planned before those 10-minutes appeared? Were you able to squeeze in some activity on most days? Did you feel better about yourself on those days when you did some exercise? Did you have more patience with your students and feel more energetic after you exercised? If you answered, "yes" to the first two questions, I have no doubt that you answered yes to all of the questions. It is amazing what a little exercise can do for your attitude, self-esteem, self-confidence, and energy levels. Even if you answered "no" to the first two questions, our vacation time provides a chance to increase the attention we give ourselves.

With each grading period in the school year, we set new goals and expectations for our students and ourselves. Think of summer as a new and stress-free grading period. What are your summer fitness goals? Do you want to get into swimsuit shape? Or are you hooked on exercise enough that your goal is to simply exercise more? Whatever the goal, we need to be intelligent in how we approach our training. Remember the track coach in Chapter 1 that yelled at his athletes, "run faster"? We don't want to simply tell you to exercise harder or more, we want to teach you how you can exercise smarter and more intensely.

PRINCIPLE TRAINING, NOT PRINCIPAL TRAINING

There are a few basic training principles that you need to keep in mind as you plan for a summer of health and fitness. These principles can help you reach your exercise goals. Is it critical that you understand and apply all of these principles? No, but remember, you want to train smarter, not just harder. These principles help you get the most for your efforts in the safest manner possible.

PRINCIPLE OF INDIVIDUAL DIFFERENCES

It is important to remember that no two people begin at the exact same fitness level or improve at the same rate. Fitness is a personal journey. Some of you reading this book are at the fitness level that would allow you to easily walk for 30 minutes and some of you might struggle walking for 5 minutes. Remember, this is not a race.

Set personal improvement goals rather than comparing yourself to others that are more fit. It is no secret that there are differences in people's abilities to improve their fitness and perform skills. While a portion of your ability is genetically predetermined, you can improve your current fitness level.

PRINCIPLE OF SPECIFICITY

This principle holds that you must match your training to your goals. Think of this principle in terms of your teaching. If you want your students to improve their addition skills, you have them practice adding numbers, not conjugating verbs. The same idea holds for exercise. If you want to improve your muscle tone, you need to do resistance training. If you want to improve your cardiovascular health, you need to walk or do some kind of aerobic activity. Any type of movement or exercise is beneficial; however, the more specific you are in your fitness goals the more specific you need to be in your training.

PRINCIPLE OF REVERSIBILITY

Another name for this principle is the "use it or lose it" principle. Think back for a moment to a computer class that you took in college. Could you jump on a computer right now and feel confident that you could use all of those programs you were taught in class? Can you even remember the names of the programs that you learned? This is a classic example of how our skills in certain areas diminish without consistent practice. This same idea applies to the adaptations that we make physically. For instance, suppose that you have worked your way up to walking two miles a day over the course of the school year. Summer hits and you decide to take a two-month vacation from walking. What do you think will happen to your ability to walk those two miles? Not only will the ease in which you could previously walk those miles be lessened, you have lost a great deal of calorie burning in the process.

At this point, you may be thinking, "Why would I want to increase my exercise in the summer when I will only lose it again once school starts and my schedule gets crazy?" What you have to remember is that maintaining your fitness level is much easier than improving it. It makes sense to work a little harder in the summer on improving your fitness and concentrate on maintaining it during the school year. And who knows, you may find yourself needing the exercise for stress management, self-confidence, or self-esteem. Once exercise is a regular part of your day, it is much easier to keep it up even when time is tight.

PRINCIPLE OF PROGRESSIVE OVERLOAD

I have a friend who consistently violates this principle. I call him the "World's Greatest Weekend Warrior." Six out of seven days a week he does no activity other than play video games and walk to the kitchen. One day a week, however, he thinks he is Michael Jordan. He goes to the local YMCA and plays full-court basketball until he collapses, which usually doesn't take long. The remainder of the week he is too tired and too sore to move off the couch or out of his chair at work. Not only is this an unhealthy way to exercise, it is dangerous and not very enjoyable.

The principle of progressive overload states that you should approach exercise in increments. Too much too soon is not advisable. Your training should be approached with small, gradual steps that allow your body to safely adapt to the increased levels of exercise.

Fitness experts use the acronym FIT to explain the subcomponents of this principle. The letters stand for frequency, intensity, and time. Each of these ideas is critical in understanding the principle of progressive overload.

- *Frequency:* How often do you exercise? Someone beginning an exercise program should not jump into training every day. The body needs time to acclimate to exercise. It is important to ease into a regular training regimen.

- *Intensity:* How hard do you exercise? Intensity deals with your heart rate and rate of respiration. Experts have identified target heart rate zones that are appropriate measures of intensity for strengthening the heart and lungs. Once you have worked up to this zone, you will greatly improve your cardiovascular health.

    Most fitness professionals advocate a target heart rate range between 60 and 85 percent of your maximal heart rate. To find your target heart rate zone, follow these steps:

    1. Determine your maximal heart rate by subtracting your age from 220. For example, if you are 35, you will subtract 35 from 220; your maximal heart rate is 185 beats per minute.

    2. Multiply your maximal rate by .60. In our example, 185 times .60 equals 111 beats per minute. This is the low end of your range.

    3. Multiply your maximal rate by .85. In our example, 185 times .85 equals 157 beats per minute. This is the high end of your range.

    4. Your target heart rate zone would be between the low and high ends of your range. In our

example, this would be between 111 and 157 beats per minute.

♦ *Time:* This term refers to the duration of your workout session. How long do you exercise? Most educators, even in summer, don't have two hours a day to devote to exercise. Furthermore, I doubt that many, if any, would really want to exercise for that length of time. The interesting thing about this component of time is that it is directly related to the component of intensity. Think in terms of walking a mile as compared to jogging a mile. Regardless if you walk or run that mile, you will burn the same amount of calories. The difference is in the amount of time that it takes to do each. Most seasoned walkers cover the distance of a mile in about 15 minutes. Most seasoned runners, however, cover the same distance in 6 to 10 minutes. You can see that by increasing the intensity of your training you can burn more calories in a shorter amount of time. It took the walker 15 minutes to burn the same amount of calories that the runner did in half the time. Although the idea of getting things done quickly is enticing, you must remember to work up to these levels of intensity. As you get in better shape, you can also increase the length of time that you exercise.

SOME SUMMERTIME MOTIVATORS

Now that you understand several principles of training, it is time to put this knowledge to use. Applying these principles to your exercise program will help make your training enjoyable and allow you to stay consistent. The ways that are available to increase your exercise pace are as limitless as your imagination. Here follows some suggestions that might help get you started.

♦ *Spice your life:* Keep your exercise program exciting by throwing in some variety from time to time. Go for a hike, try in-line skating or cycling, visit a state park and take a canoe tour; park a mile away from your favorite ice-cream shop, walk there, enjoy some fat-free ice cream, and walk back to your car.

♦ *Make a $15 commitment:* Sometimes all it takes to reignite our motivation is having something new. Purchasing something directly related to our exercise goals gives us a new and exciting starting point. Maybe a new CD to play while you work out in the living room will be enough to get you back on track. How about a new exercise outfit that makes you feel good about your "physique in transformation"? Whatever you choose to buy, make sure that it means something to you. If the *Rocky* soundtrack doesn't motivate you, don't waste your money on it. Find something that triggers a memory about a time when you felt great about yourself and use it for exercise fuel.

♦ *Join a fitness facility:* There are several motivating factors that accompany joining a gym. Membership fees usually provide some amount of motivation to get to the gym so that your money is not wasted. Another important source of motivation comes from being in an environment where everyone is exercising.

♦ *Hire a personal trainer:* Many people choose to hire a personal trainer to help keep them motivated in their training. There is something comforting about knowing that you are working with a professional and that your time and efforts are not wasted. Having a personal trainer also adds a degree of accountability to your workouts. It is much harder to skip a workout when someone is waiting for you to show up. The amount of money that you pay your personal trainer can also be a motivating factor in keeping you on your routine.

Being healthy is a lifetime commitment. Sometimes it requires a little imagination to stay consistent. Use the previous suggestions, or find your own, and combine them with your knowledge of the principles of training and you will be on your way to feeling great.

PART IV

FINDING A FIT
FOR YOU

10

EVERYBODY HAS BEEN ON A DIET— WHAT WILL WORK FOR ME?

We all know that if one diet worked for everyone, we'd all be on one diet. Finding a strategy that best fits you is one of the keys to successful weight loss and control. There are many books, articles, and ideas for many diets, but finding one that works for you is the key. Let's examine some ideas that may be a fit for you.

THE FAD DIET

Almost any magazine you pick up has an article about losing 15 pounds in a week or 25 pounds by Christmas, and so on. It is easy to be skeptical, especially when some of these same magazines contain such headlines as "Psychic's Head Explodes."

However, rather than just completely disregard any short-term diets, it might be better to ask a few questions. What should we do with this information? Should we just pitch them because they all are silly? Or should we jump from one to another to another? There is no easy answer to these questions (and you already knew that didn't you), but let's think through some aspects of a quick weight-loss diet.

One thing we do know is that you need to burn 3,500 more calories than you take in to lose one pound and if you consume 3,500 more calories than you use, then you will gain a pound. It really is that simple. If you normally live on and maintain your weight with a 2,500-calorie diet and you cut that down to 1,800 calories and continue to burn at the same rate, you will lose one pound every five days. Though the scales may show more because of water loss and some other factors, this is essentially the rate that you are dropping. Understand though, you can only drop one pound every five days for as long as you consume at this lower level. With fad diets, you must ask, How long can I continue to eat this way? If you return to your previous habits after the diet is over, then the weight will return also. Additionally, there could be health implications, such as the risk of muscle loss.

Yet, we are not going to simply dismiss all the diet plans you may see. For some people they may be a great jump start to changing a life style. These benefits and immediate changes can be even more dramatic and significant if coupled with the beginnings of a new exercise program.

There may be people in the world who can change the way they eat or exercise gradually and have the patience to weigh themselves once every six weeks and be happy with one pound every month or so. Realistically, though, most people are anxious to see some initial results on a much quicker basis. Though it would be difficult to maintain any kind of a dramatic reduction in food intake in perpetuity, if the quick results can energize you into making a more appropriate shift into a long-term exercise and healthy eating program, then it is not inherently a bad idea. Even if it is mostly a water loss, if dropping five pounds quickly is the incentive you need at the start of a program to live in a more healthy manner, then that is enough of a reason to consider trying to jump-start your program with a fad diet that appeals to you.

I am not sure any of us could live on cabbage or a particular sub sandwich forever, but if dropping weight quickly empowers us to make lifelong changes, then it is something to consider. And though we should always be aware of potential health risks of a diet, not changing the way we eat and live may be the biggest risk of all. Many fad diets do not provide the balanced nutrition we need. But then, neither does many of the daily diets that so many of us regularly eat.

There are many less-dramatic alternatives to a totally controlled diet. These may well be easier to maintain over the long haul. Different people can live with different kinds of plans and approaches. As always, the trick is to find the trick that works for you. Let's take a look at some of those. If you can find a way to just shave off even a few calories on a regular basis over time, it will make a dramatic difference that you can sustain throughout your life.

Again, there is no one size fits all approach. And, additionally, variety may be a needed component in order to maintain the energy and momentum you need to lead a healthier lifestyle. So, rather than just discount articles you see on "Miracle Weight-Loss Plans," it is okay to see if there are any aspects of it that might be a good fit for you.

THE STOP EATING AFTER 6:30 IDEA

Rather than completely shifting every item we eat, if we can just change some aspects, then we might be much more able to alter our bodies forever. One example is setting a certain time in the evening to stop eating. Not eating after supper or not eating after 6:30 PM may be a reasonable goal for you. It is also a nice approach because then you feel thinner each morning (and look it too!), which can set a positive tone for each day's food choices. This can be appropriate because it can allow you to have a variety during the day and with your meals, but it is a clear ending point in terms of food consumption each day.

Another approach would be to limit the types of food you have after a certain time. In other words, rather than eating nothing after supper, at least limit your after-supper choices to only healthy items such as celery, and so on. This way you do not completely shut the eating off, but force yourself to eat in a better way at least part of the day. This will be especially beneficial if you are in the habit of late evening snacks of higher calorie foods. This change will give you flexibility during the day but can create a long-term change in your eating and your appearance.

CHANGING BEVERAGE SELECTIONS

One of the first things I did when I changed my exercise and eating lifestyle was to give up regular soda. If you consume any beverage with calories, there are many low/no calorie substitutes available. Whole milk can be replaced by 2 percent milk or, better yet, skim milk. Sugar, cream, and caffeine can all be left out or reduced in coffee or lattes. Almost all beverages have diet alternatives. Although the initial transition may be a challenge—when I gave up caffeine, I had headaches for a week—it is the kind of change that can make a permanent difference in our caloric consumption and weight.

JUST A TASTE

One of the things that many people suffer from is cravings. We all have our weaknesses. It may be pizza, or donuts, or chocolate. Yours may be something less traditional. However, an approach that may allow you to fill these desires and yet eat in a more healthy manner is to make a deal with yourself. Agree that you can have your favorite candy bar, but only eat half of it. Instead of ordering a whole pizza, find a place that you can order by the slice. If you know you will allow yourself to have your favorites if you do so in selected amounts, it may accomplish the goal of scratching that craving itch, but not cause undue harm to your healthy lifestyle efforts.

If normally you eat two donuts after church, allow yourself one. If typically you reach in and grab five of your favorite cookies out of the pantry don't completely deny, but settle for two or three. Making these deals with yourself can strike a nice compromise between enjoying life and enjoying yourself.

IT'S NO MORE EXPENSIVE
TO PITCH IT THAN TO EAT IT

One thing that I have learned is that it is no more expensive to buy something and only eat part of it than it is to buy something and eat all of it. If the only way to get the taste of that pizza you are really desiring is to buy an entire pie, then go ahead, but agree that you will throw out half of it rather than eat it all. It may seem wasteful, but it is much better than feeling bad after you wolf it all down. If you are like me, when you throw it away you better put it in some real garbage so that you are not tempted to salvage it later!

We probably all spent a great deal of our childhood being reminded to clean our plates and to not waste any food. I was told on many occasions how lucky I was to have this food and that I needed to eat every bite. Those guilt pangs may still reverberate within us, but whether we eat every bite or throw part away, no one else was going to get any of it anyhow. You accomplish two goals when you agree to do this before you order something. You feel less guilty about cheating on your eating plan; and you feel less guilty about the amount of higher calorie food you consumed.

REMEMBER HOW YOU'LL FEEL TOMORROW

We had discussed earlier that one of our keys to exercise is to remember how you'll feel when you are done, before you even start. Well, this same idea applies to eating better. If you can shift away from thinking how good this cheesecake is going to taste to focusing on "How will I feel about this tomorrow," it may allow you to make better choices.

I oftentimes try to think of upcoming events where I want to try to look my best—reunions, holiday parties, important meetings—and if I can do this before eating that extra pastry, I often make better decisions and feel much better about my decisions. If you can make this a regular habit, then it can become a way of life that can really make a difference over time.

THE CEREAL APPROACH

One thing that is helpful to me is to find foods that I really like and that are good for me—or at least not too negative—and eat them as small meals several times a day. During the summer, peaches are one of my favorites. If, in mid-morning or afternoon or even in the evening, I can choose to eat a delicious peach instead of a candy bar, then I am making a positive choice. Not only is it better in terms of calories and fat, but it is filling enough that it will reduce the amount I will eat at my next meal. You probably have positive foods that come to mind that can serve this purpose for you. Pretzels, carrots, and many other items can fill that role. A recent favorite that I have is cereal.

The reason that I have found cereal to be a great small meal substitute is because it is low in calories and fat (especially with skim milk) and there is an incredible variety. You can meet the need of a sweet tooth, feel healthy about your choice, or just have a childhood favorite. Not only does cereal come in many tastes and types, generally it is also very filling. Even two or three bowls typically do not have a great deal of calories and fat. Additionally, if you choose the right brands, you may be able to add significant nutritional benefits to your diet. Foods like this can serve a critical link in making long-term positive changes in your eating habits.

And if you feel that you would get tired of one food repetitively, identify five or six favorites and have them around, or rotate them frequently as your snacks or mini-meals. If you combine this idea with the idea we just discussed in the "Just a Taste" section, your strategy can be doubly effective.

If I am heading out to a restaurant where I'll be tempted to greatly overeat or to a party with many taste-tempting-but-oh-so-bad-for-you snacks, before I go I will eat a bowl of cereal or two. This is a positive alternative, but does not fill me up to the point that I won't enjoy tasting my favorites at the social gathering. However, it will also keep me from being so hungry that I will stuff myself with less than positive food choices.

Whether it is fruit, vegetables, yogurt, cereal, or whatever your healthy favorite is, determining something that you can regularly tap into can be of great support as you look to make long-range growth in your fitness and weight-loss programs.

DON'T COMPOUND YOUR MISTAKES—GET BACK ON TRACK

One error that can really bring us down is to go off course in terms of eating—or exercise for that matter—and then simply give up. Or worse yet, we compound an error by eating a box of cookies to console ourselves. Well, everyone makes mistakes. So what if you messed up? Who cares? What we are promoting in this book is a life change; any mistakes from this point of view are minor when compared to your lifelong goals. Just forget about them and move back to doing what is right.

If taking a day off from running energizes you even more, then it is okay. You know yourself best. Even if you skip two weeks, it is not too late to get back on track. You are making life-changing decisions, and no matter what, don't let a small or temporary mistake—or even a big, colossal one—keep you from doing the right thing over time.

11

GUIDELINES FOR EATING HEALTHY

One theme that surfaces frequently in this book is the importance of balance: in your work and play, in your self-care and care for others, and in the foods you eat. Food is energy for the body. It is important to eat a wide variety of foods to ensure that your body receives all the essential nutrients for growth and maintenance. It is also important to strike a balance between food intake and your expenditure of calories. If weight loss is your main concern, then you must expend more calories than you consume. The balance comes in understanding the importance that certain foods play in your health and wellness.

THE SIX ESSENTIAL NUTRIENTS

The body requires six essential nutrients to function. These nutrients are protein, carbohydrates, fats, minerals, vitamins, and water. Only three of the six provide the body with energy. Protein, carbohydrates, and fats are the body's energy sources. Vitamins, minerals, and water provide no energy but are necessary for the proper functioning of the body. If you are in search of a healthy body, you must have all six of the essential nutrients in the proper proportion.

JUST THE FACTS...PLEASE!

The goal of this chapter is to help educators make intelligent decisions regarding food choices. You don't have to be a nutritionist to design a healthy meal plan, but you must have some basic facts. The first aspect of any diet is understanding how many calories you need. The number of calories needed each day depends upon the body's metabolic rate. Your metabolic rate depends on factors such as sex, age, body size, muscle mass, glandular function, and exercise. There are many methods of calculating your caloric needs, all of which vary in complexity. But you must have a method of at least approximating your caloric needs. The following is a simple method for estimating your basal metabolic rate (BMR). Your BMR is your metabolic rate at rest. It is the amount of calories that you need to support all body functions, including respiration, heart rate, body temperature, and blood pressure.

- *Males:* Divide your body weight by 2.2 then multiply by 24. For example, a 175-lb male's body weight (175) divided by 2.2 and multiplied 24 equals 1,909 calories.

- *Females:* Multiply your body weight by .95, then divide by 2.2 and multiply by 24. For example, a 120-lbs female's body weight (120) times .95, then divided by 2.2 and multiplied by 24 equals 1,244.

Your BMR provides a starting point in determining how many calories you need on a daily basis. Understanding this concept allows you to modify your caloric intake to accomplish your fitness goals. Let me provide you with some additional examples.

- If a person has a high percentage of body fat that they want to lower while toning their existing muscles, they should eat 1.5 times their BMR on days when they exercise. They should try to stay close to their actual BMR caloric needs on days in which they don't exercise.

- If a person has an average amount of body fat which they want to lower while toning their existing muscles, they should double their BMR on days which they exercise. They should consume 1.5 times their BMR on days in which they don't exercise.

- If a person has low body fat and wants to build or tone their muscles, they should double their BMR each day.

It is important to remember, however, that your BMR is your resting metabolic rate. It doesn't take into account any of your daily activity. Any activity that you do during the day will impact your caloric needs. If your BMR is 2,000 calories and you expend 300 calories during the day walking around your classroom and the school building, you are already 300 calories in debt. This means that you could consume 2,300 calories without gaining any weight. Beware of consuming too few calories. Most people forget to account for their daily activity when determining caloric needs. Your BMR is the least amount of calories that you should consume! Remember food is our ally not our enemy.

The bottom line, however, is that what matters in gaining or losing weight is how *much* we eat. If you eat more than you expend you gain weight. If you eat less than you expend you lose weight. Although *what* you eat plays a minor role in weight gain or loss, it plays a major role in your overall health.

Let me give you an example. Let's say that yesterday was a very busy day for me and in all of my running around I only had time to grab a Big Mac and a large fries from McDonalds. My caloric intake total for the day would be 939 calories. If my caloric needs to maintain my current body weight is 2,200 calories, I would lose weight if I continued to only consume 939 calories. The problem of not monitoring what you eat, however, is not as obvious. A Big Mac and large fries has a fat total of 45 grams; 14 of which come from saturated fat. High amounts of saturated fat in a diet are linked to increased risk for chronic diseases such as heart disease and some forms of cancer. Remember, its not just about losing weight, its about losing weight in a healthy manner.

HOW DO I LOSE WEIGHT
IN A HEALTHY MANNER?

The healthiest way to lose weight is slowly. One to two pounds of loss per week is a healthy goal. Think of your diet in terms of one pound of fat being equal to 3,500 calories. If you can finish each day of the week with a 500-calorie deficit, you will lose one pound at the end of seven days. A 500-calorie deficit is not that difficult to do if it is done with the combination of lowering your caloric intake and increasing your exercise. Here is a personal example. I love Oreo cookies! In fact, I love them so much that I eat them almost every day for a snack. If I wanted to lose one pound in the next week, I could do so by decreasing my intake by 250 calories (or five Oreo cookies) and walking for 20 minutes each day (approximately 250 calories for me). Now that is a realistic way to lose weight! These small imbalances in intake and expenditure add up over time.

ENERGY-PRODUCING NUTRIENTS

Carbohydrates are the body's main source of energy. They should comprise approximately 40 percent of your total daily calories. Every gram of carbohydrate provides four calories. There are two main types of carbohydrates, simple and complex. Complex carbohydrates are recommended over simple ones because they are digested more slowly and may decrease the risk of obesity, heart disease, and diabetes. Examples of complex carbohydrates include fruits, vegetables, whole-grain breads, and cereals. Simple carbohydrates are sugars such as fructose, glucose, sucrose, lactose, and maltose. These sugars are commonly found in candy and soft drinks.

Protein is another energy-producing nutrient. Protein intake should be approximately 30 percent of your total daily calories. Every gram of protein provides four calories. Protein provides the building blocks for all of the body's cells. Proteins are formed from 22 amino acids. Fourteen of these amino acids are formed naturally in your body. The remaining eight must be obtained through food. Foods from animal sources such as fish, meat, eggs, chicken, and dairy products provide all eight essential amino acids and are called complete proteins. Examples of incomplete proteins are nuts, rice, and beans.

The third energy-producing nutrient is fat. Fat intake should comprise approximately 30 percent of your total daily calories. Approximately 20 percent should come from mono- and polyunsaturated fats and less than 10 percent should come from saturated fats. Saturated fats are typically solid at room temperature and come primarily from animal sources. Unsaturated fats are typically liquid at room temperature and come primarily form plant sources. Fat is higher in calories than carbohydrates and protein. Each gram of fat provides nine calories.

The body needs carbohydrates, proteins, and fats to function. A healthy diet contains all three of these nutrients in the proper proportions. Cutting fat completely out of your diet, for instance, is not a healthy way to lose weight. Again, balance is the key to healthy weight loss.

THE GOOD, THE BAD, AND THE UGLY OF FOOD CHOICES!

There are healthy and unhealthy choices regarding each of the three energy-producing nutrients. The following lists should give you some direction in the types of foods that are good for you and the ones that you should try to avoid.

- ◆ Carbohydrates—healthy choices

   Brown rice, red potatoes, oatmeal, barley, rye, apples, grapes, grapefruit, peas, lima beans, soy beans, yogurt, and any green vegetable.

- ◆ Carbohydrates—poor choices

   Candy, potato chips, most breads, soft drinks, desserts, and baked goods.

- ◆ Proteins—healthy choices

   Chicken breast (skinless), lean beef, lean turkey, tuna in spring water, cod, egg whites, and tofu.

- ◆ Proteins—poor choices

   Most beef and sausages, pepperoni, beacon, and hot dogs.

- ◆ Fats—healthy choices

   Monounsaturated fats including olive oil, peanut oil, and canola oil.

- ◆ Fats—poor choices

   High saturated fats including butter, mayonnaise, sour cream, and hydrogenated oils.

If you are thinking that you will never be able to enjoy that Oreo Sundae again…relax! You can still eat the foods that you enjoy and desire. The trick is to do it in moderation. If you can keep healthy foods as the bulk of your diet you can, from time to time, enjoy the not so healthy foods. Remember, a healthy diet is about *balance*.

12

FAD OR FACT? WHAT DIETS REALLY WORK?

It seems as though a new "miracle diet" hits the bookstores or the infomercials almost on a daily basis. With such information overload, it is easy to understand why many people feel lost as to which diets they should try. As we discussed in Chapter 10, we believe that there is no one best diet for everyone. People react differently to the various diet approaches. This chapter will provide you with some basic information regarding the most popular fad diets. When it comes to choosing a healthy diet plan, a little knowledge goes a long way.

I always suggest to my clients that they ask two questions when choosing a diet plan. First, "Do the results that the diet is claiming to produce sound realistic?" It is important to listen to that little voice in your head that says, "That sounds too good to be true." In regard to quick-fix diets, that voice is usually correct. A diet that claims you will lose 35 pounds in two weeks is not healthy or realistic. The second question that should be asked is, "Is this diet something that I can live with?" Can you stay on the proposed nutrition plan for a lifetime? I don't know about you, but the idea of eating grapefruit two meals a day for the rest of my life is not appealing! The problem with most diets is that they are designed with the quick fix in mind and they don't teach healthy eating habits. Most people who try these diets lose a few pounds only to later resume their old eating habits and gain more pounds than they previously lost. This is called the yo-yo effect or rebounding, and is a common occurrence in fad-dieters. When people put extreme restrictions on what they eat and the calories that they consume, the body will reciprocate by slowing down the rate at which it burns calories.

We mentioned in Chapter 10, however, that fad diets should not be dismissed all together. If they provide you a jump start on weight loss and you understand that it is unhealthy and unrealistic to remain on one for an extended period of time, its utility is justified. It is always easier to stick with something once you have seen results. If a fad diet helps you to drop 10 pounds and it makes you feel better about yourself, you are much more likely to try and eat healthy and exercise to continue to feel good about your body.

Fad diets are much easier to understand if we classify them into two general categories. The two categories that have enjoyed the most popularity recently are diets high in carbohydrates and low in fat and diets that are low in carbohydrates and high in protein. While both approaches have their unique focus, they all have at their core a foundation of consuming lower calories. Some advocate using precise calorie counts each meal while others base the serving on what can fit in the palm of their hand. Another common feature of most fad diets is a concentration on certain foods considered good, while limiting or eliminating the foods considered to be bad.

LOW CARBOHYDRATE– HIGH PROTEIN APPROACH

Diets using this approach are by far the most popular ones today. This popularity stems from several sources, some legitimate and some not. Low carbohydrate–high protein diets often boast of producing rapid weight loss, sometimes in excess of 10 pounds in one week. Is that possible? It is possible, but the weight loss comes initially from a loss of water not a loss of fat. Over time, however, this approach can reduce a person's body fat. Diets in this category are based on two main ideas. First, protein is harder for the body to digest than carbohydrates. More calories are expended in breaking the protein down into a usable form of energy than with carbohydrates. Secondly, this approach attempts to eliminate most forms of sugar. Refined sugar and other carbohydrates are often credited for causing weight gain. Simple carbohydrates such as soft drinks and candy bars offer little, if any, nutritional value while being high in calories.

While some people have achieved success with this approach, there are several health concerns surrounding it of which you should be informed. Often diets high in protein are also high in saturated fat, which is directly related to heart disease and some forms of cancer. In addition, these diets tend to be too low in fiber and calcium. Fiber is a critical part of any diet. It has been shown to reduce total blood cholesterol and may be responsible for lowering the risk of diabetes mellitus and hypertension. Calcium is essential in building strong bones and teeth. If you do not consume adequate amounts of calcium, you may become susceptible to osteoporosis. Osteoporosis occurs when bone mass decreases to very low levels.

HIGH CARBOHYDRATE– LOW FAT APPROACH

This approach focuses on eating generous helpings of carbohydrates while limiting the amount of fat consumed. This is a much more healthy way of eating than the low carbohydrate-high protein approach. The problem with the high carbohydrate–low fat approaches, however, is that they often give the impression that you should eat large portions of carbohydrates and severely limit or eliminate fat in your diet. Both of these assumptions are incorrect. How much you eat, even if it is complex carbohydrates, matters in weight loss. If you consume more calories than you expend, you gain weight. Sound familiar, does it? This approach also gives the impression that all fat is bad. We have already discussed that fat is essential in your diet. What is most important is that you don't overconsume fat and that the majority of your dietary fat comes from unsaturated sources.

Carbohydrates are your body's main source of fuel. If your diet contains a bulk of complex carbohydrates that are high in fiber and low in sugar, you will be lowering your chances for developing chronic diseases. Both the low carbohydrate–high protein diet and the high carbohydrate–low fat diet have weight-loss potential. Any diet taken to extreme measures, however, is potentially dangerous to your health. Exercise moderation if you chose one of these approaches. A well-balanced diet with a variety of foods will achieve the same results as these fad diets, only without the health risks.

FORGET THE FAD DIET— WHAT ABOUT DIET PILLS?

Diet pills and fat-burners seem to be the approach of choice for our high-speed society. Who wouldn't want the convenience of swallowing a pill that will not only reduce your appetite but also increase your metabolism? Remember that little voice that alerts us to things that sound too good to be true? Is it talking to you now? These pills do work, for a short time. More important, however, are the health risks associated with these supplements.

The majority of diet pills contain nervous system stimulants such as ephedrine and caffeine. While these substances increase your body's rate of fat burning, they also increase your heart rate and blood pressure. These stimulants have been linked to several deaths. If you suffer from any heart disease or hypertension, you should completely avoid all diet and energy supplements.

Diet pills decrease your appetite by slowing the movement of food through your digestive system. This gives you the feeling of being full for longer than normal periods. The supplement's ability to slow the movement of food only lasts for about two weeks. The body, after two weeks, adapts to the supplement and actually reverses its effects. The movement of food through your digestive tract will be increased. This gives you the feeling of being empty and increases your appetite. In periods of extended use, these supplements actually work against your dieting efforts.

There are no miracle diets. Some will help you lose a few pounds quickly, but, in the end, it comes down to eating a wide variety of foods in moderation. When a balanced diet is coupled with a consistent exercise program, a healthy weight loss will occur.

13

STAYING ON TRACK!

As an educator, you understand the importance of motivation. You constantly strive to motivate your students to achieve and you understand that what motivates one student might not motivate another. Health and fitness are lifetime commitments, and, as with any long-term commitment, you will have periods of highs and lows. Understanding what personally motivates you is critical in keeping you on track—with fitness or any other endeavor. Look at teaching for example. Reflect back upon your teaching. I bet you can recall several times—sometimes days, sometimes even months long—when you felt unmotivated. It seemed as though it was all you could do to make it to 3:30 PM. But you did make it. Why? Chances are it was because you were able to use a source of inspiration to make it through the tough times. As educators, we have many sources of inspiration sitting in our classrooms. That is part of what makes teaching so rewarding, and it also enables you to continue to give to your students.

You have to make a similar connection in regard to your health and fitness. What are sources of inspiration that will help you stay on track with your physical self-care? Your motivation might come from knowing that you are healthy and better able to care for your family. Maybe the motivation comes from the increased energy that goes along with exercising. This extra positive energy is then transferred to other areas of your life and to your family, students, and friends. Or does the motivation stem from knowing that you look better? It doesn't matter the source of the motivation as long as you know what it is and that it is personal. Most successful people have a firm understanding as to what motivates them to stay committed to their goals.

Once you have identified your source of inspiration or motivation, it is time to get specific about how you can program in reminders, checks, and rewards. Most educators believe in preparation. How many times have we said, "Failing to prepare is preparing to fail?" The same energy and strategic thinking that you put into your lesson plans should be put into your fitness plan. This doesn't mean that you have to write every workout down on paper and keep meticulous notes regarding the sets, weights, and repetitions that you performed. It simply means that you should have an outline of where you want to go and how you are going to get there.

Plan on a few detours and maybe a flat tire or two along the way. If you have prepared for these things in advance, they tend to seem much less devastating. These detours and flat tires are only minor setbacks in your training or diet. Maybe you made some poor food choices at the cafeteria. Think of it as a detour and get right back on track eating healthy at your next meal. Many people feel as though if they eat one unhealthy meal they have ruined their diet and they are tempted to continue to eat poorly for several meals. If the road you are driving upon takes a detour, do you take off aimlessly on your own detour because you are already off course? Or do you follow the detour signs and get back to your original route as quickly as possible? The same idea applies to your eating and training. Missing one workout does not ruin all of your previous training. It may, in fact, be beneficial. Think of it in terms of resting your body so you can have a great workout tomorrow.

AVOIDING THE TEMPTATIONS

Reminders, checks, and rewards are all part of staying on track in your diet and exercise program. These are small, but very important, things that you can use to help keep you motivated and to reward you for your hard work. For these to work, however, they must be simple and have some personal connection for you. Let's examine the roles that reminders, checks, and rewards play in your success.

REMINDERS

Reminders are pictures, symbols, notes, or quotes that are strategically placed to remind you of your goals. These are very powerful when they have some personal connection driving them. A friend of mine uses a picture of herself when she was very physically fit. It is a picture of her in a tank top and shorts with a big smile on her face. She tells me that the picture reminds her how great she felt when she was in shape. This picture hangs on her mirror in her bedroom.

Another example of a reminder is a quote I once saw on a friend's refrigerator that read, "Are you really hungry, or are you just checking to see if the light still works?" He used this sign to break his habit of going to the fridge whenever he passed through the kitchen.

Any quote that empowers you to take control of your time and your life are helpful in keeping you on track in your fitness and diet routines. I know of one teacher who has a quote on the inside of her planner that states, "How will I use my P.T. today?" She explained to me that her P.T. was her personal time. The note reminded her to take advantage of the small breaks of time during her day. It is easy to see how those little opportunities could be missed without such a reminder.

Find a quote or a picture that has some significance to you and place where you will see it at a critical time during your day. Let it serve as a reminder of something that you should be doing or something that you should try to avoid.

CHECKS

Checks are previously determined daily, weekly, or monthly goals that you want to achieve. These goals can be written or kept in your head, whatever works best for you. Their purpose is to keep you on track in working to achieve specific results. It is important to keep these goals flexible. If your goals seem too difficult or too easy upon reflection, adjust them accordingly. An example of a weekly check I use is the following list:

♦ Do some form of cardiovascular exercise for 30 minutes, four days this week.

+ Weight train three times this week.

+ Eat fast food no more than two meals this week.

Your checks, like your reminders, need to be personal. It is important that you make your checks realistic. If there is no chance that you will go a week without eating fast food, then don't set that as a goal. You want to be successful in the challenges that are realistic. If, however, you don't succeed in meeting your goals, you should learn something from them. Checks should provide guidance in determining realistic goals and point out where those reminders might be most useful.

REWARDS

Rewards signify accomplishments and reinforce desired behaviors. When it comes to meeting your health and fitness goals, you deserve to be rewarded! It is important to set rewards for meeting certain goals. If walking three days a week is a challenge for you, then give yourself a reward for accomplishing that goal. Rewards provide incentives for reaching those goals that are more difficult to attain.

The challenge is to find healthy rewards. Our society typically celebrates accomplishments with food. While there is nothing wrong with using food as a reward, it should only be one of many choices. If knowing that you can have that Oreo sundae on Friday is enough to make you walk every day this week...go for it! However, it is beneficial to have some of your rewards linked to your fitness activities. If you enjoy walking while listening to music, for instance, buy a favorite CD when you reach a certain goal. If you have a movie that really motivates you to exercise, reward yourself with a movie night. (Grading papers is not allowed.) Maybe a new pair of shoes or a workout outfit would be a nice reward. Now you can justify those little indulgences that you have denied yourself. Remember, you deserve it!

Being healthy is a way of life. You have already completed the most difficult part...getting started. Don't let a little slip here and there stop you from continuing to improve your fitness. Use the guidelines presented in this chapter and develop your own reminders, checks, and rewards to keep yourself on track to a more healthy you!

14

SUMMING IT ALL UP

Whew, it was a workout just reading the book! Well, congratulations, you made it. Now, you know what to do and hopefully you are well on your way to a better you. You have focused on ways to eat better and burn more calories through exercise. And, maybe most importantly, you have determined some ways to make it all work for you. Maybe you can only free up 10 minutes at a time. Now you know how to use that time to better yourself. We have also been reminded why it is so essential for educators to take care of ourselves. We give so much to others, it is critical that we give some back to ourselves.

Teachers are master motivators. We learn how to impact and encourage even our most resistant students. And, really, the more challenging the student, the more satisfaction we get when we feel we have made a difference. We have also realized that this same thing applies to ourselves. The less we like to exercise the more we have to focus on finding ways that will work for us. And, the greater the impact we can have as a role model. Just as anyone can teach the valedictorian and feel good about it, the student with less natural ability needs us more than the more gifted. Being able to turn these motivational abilities internally is an essential piece of feeling our best.

If our goal is accomplished, then you are chomping at the bit to get started. We hope you were hitting the treadmill or putting down that candy bar before you even reached this point. However, if you are interested, but can not quite get started, then try this.

THE HOUR RULE

Many organizations have what they call *hour rules*. What this means is that they believe that if you hear of a good idea or get motivated to do something then you must act upon it within a certain number of hours or you probably will never follow up. For example, a 72-hour rule means that if you do not act on something—say, perhaps, you don't go right out and buy that new gizmo—within the next 72 hours, then you probably never will. The same is probably true for the ideas in this book, no matter how great they seem to you right now. So, set a guideline for yourself; say to yourself right now that within 24 hours you will do some type of exercise. Then follow through on this promise to yourself and do it. You know from reading this far that even the smallest action will do as a start. And then, make a commitment that, no matter what, you will do something—*anything*—for the next three days.

Three days from now, sit back, enjoy that cool of the evening feeling, and realize that you can feel this great every day. And, remember, you cannot get "in shape," whatever that means, in three days. But you'll understand that this is a life commitment you are making.

IT'S NOT EITHER-OR—IT'S BOTH

Two of the major sections in this book are focused on fitness and diet. Although we divided them within the book, it is really not one *or* the other. It is really one *and* the other. The most powerful change you can make is a fusion of having a better diet combined with increasing your exercise level. Blending these two approaches can help you improve how you feel and look faster than either approach taken alone. More importantly, blending these approaches can help you sustain and maintain any changes that you make.

Financial advisors recommend a diversified portfolio. They remind us that when stocks go down, bonds can go up. Having things that go up when others go down can, over the long term, create balanced growth through good and bad financial times. Over the long term, you end up better off. This same thing is true when you combine diet and exercise.

The holiday seasons are often the most challenging times to watch what you eat. If you approach the winter festivities with this in mind, you can sustain your fitness level by increasing your exercise during this time. And, the opposite is also true. If at some point you turn your ankle or are not able to exercise for a few days, if you cut back on what you eat during this time, you will still be able to feel good about your weight when you get back to your workouts. Using both diet and exercise adds the element of variety to routines. For example, you can emphasize exercise for a while or focus more closely on diet for a couple of weeks.

Even more importantly, people who have multiple ways to improve their fitness level are much less likely to go into a prolonged downturn. Interestingly, the more you weigh the more calories you burn when you run or walk a mile. Thus if you keep up the level of your exercise, you will be consuming more calories if your weight goes up slightly. And, when you return to a focus on both diet and exercise your gains can become even more rapid.

It's Balance

Just as blending diet and exercise can lead to a healthier lifestyle and a more positive appearance, balancing work and a focus on yourself can create the same feelings. It is essential that educators do their best at work. However, it is very difficult to do this on a long-term basis unless you can find that same balance between work and your personal life. Make sure that you give yourself the same energy and enthusiasm you give to your students. Not only will this make you a better teacher, it will also make you a better person. You have to make sure that you take care of yourself or there is little chance you can take care of others. Your students need you, but they need you healthy.

Best wishes as you move along the path toward eating better, exercising smarter, and feeling your best. You are worth it.